Coming Clean

My Letter-Writing Journey

Sarah Dean

ISBN: 978-1-61658-590-7

Book design by Beth Wright, Trio Bookworks
Cover and author photographs by Christopher D. Burnett, PhD

This book was printed on FSC-certified paper, with 30 percent recycled content.

Printed by McNaughton & Gunn
Print coordination by Globe Printing, Ishpeming, Michigan

FSC
Mixed Sources
Product group from well-managed
forests and other controlled sources

Cert no. SW-COC-002283
www.fsc.org
© 1996 Forest Stewardship Council

Printed in the USA

To my "boys,"
in the order of their appearance in my life:
Jonathon,
Christopher,
and Strider.
You're in my heart forever.
I love you!

Contents

To Those Who Supported My Letter-Writing Journey

Every book has a section for acknowledgments, right? So this book, being a collection of letters, has a thank-you note.

Thank You . . .

Thank you to everyone who has ever given me a journal or pen. I have loved and appreciated your gifts. Thank you, Dad, for giving me my first diary at age six. You started me on my writing path, which has been the source of much healing and growth throughout my life.

Thank you to all my faithful correspondents. I have loved sharing life with you via letters. Thank you, Mom, for being my most faithful correspondent through the years. You've always encouraged me to write thank-you notes and letters from camp or vacations.

Thank you to everyone who has listened to me share my letters—especially Jonathon, the first to read the entire book. Christopher, thank you for listening and for hearing. Helen, thank you for the writing workshops and Creativity Consultations. You have been wind beneath my wings. Thank you, Soul Sister Deanna, for being a role model of extreme honesty and my proofreader for truth. Thank you, Jon, for "box testing" my letters with the Arbinger Institute principles. And thank you, Patrick, for your support and endorsement.

Thank you, Ya Yas and Camilla, for witnessing my letter-writing journey this year. I have deeply appreciated your loving support of the process.

Thank you to the Joy Center and the Shalom Service, and to Helen and Martha, for creating sacred spaces for my initial public readings of my letter to my biological mom. Reading that letter out loud was the impetus for sharing my letters in a published book format.

Thank you to all the other people, places, and events that have called forth my writer self. I am grateful for all the encouragement and support I have received.

With heartfelt appreciation,
Sarah

To You, the Reader

Dear Reader,

Hello! Welcome to my book of letters. I have written these with you in mind. This started as an individual spiritual journey to help me heal and move past "stuck places" in my life. As a woman approaching forty, I found that I wanted to move into this next phase of my life feeling purified of any heaviness from my past. The idea to write these letters came as an answer to creating a "bucket list." I didn't have any places I *had* to visit or possessions I *needed* to acquire before I kicked the bucket. I did, however, have a desire for inner peace about my past: relationships, places, and events.

As I began to write and contemplate what I would include, you (yes, YOU) came to mind. I began to imagine you reading these letters, you being moved by some of the similarities in our lives. I imagined you feeling inspired because of what you read here and having a courageous conversation with someone or writing a completion letter of your own. I saw myself reading some of my letters out loud. I saw your heart opening to new possibilities and expanding in love.

I am so glad we're meeting in this way! Letters have always been one of my very favorite ways to communicate, both to myself (in the form of diaries and journals) and to others (thank-you letters, letters from camp, love letters, etc.). Even though most of my letters are now through e-mail, I still appreciate the power of the written word.

For some of the more challenging letters, there were many drafts. In the first attempts, I allowed myself to just vomit on the page—whatever needed to come out came out. Then I'd read over the letter for what was true and not just a story I created about the event or person. I'd think about what I would really want to say from my deathbed, to complete my relationship with this person or event. Sometimes, I'd journal about the letter and how difficult it was to write what I wanted to say, including both honesty and compassion. I'd often receive a "message" from a part of myself with a new perspective on the situation that allowed me to complete the letter with integrity and intention.

Sometimes, I realized that the letter that needed to be written was not to another person or event, but to a part of myself. So you'll notice two basic types of letters in this book: letters to others and letters to myself. I believe in the Buddhist concept of Right Relationships. And I believe Right Relationship with Self is just as important as Right Relationship with Other. We need both kinds in order to live fully, with open hearts and minds in this world. Sometimes it is enough for me to come clean with myself and reconnect to a part of myself that is out of sorts. When I do, the troubled relationship or memory seems to heal on its own. Sometimes I also need to have a courageous conversation with someone or write a letter (which I sometimes send and sometimes don't) to the other person, event, or place. I write both kinds of letters and have included both in this book.

Other letters are not necessarily about troubled relationships or difficult memories at all. Instead, they are to people or places I want to thank. In my active, healthy relationships, I try to do this in person. But some people from my past are no longer a part of my life. I wouldn't want to die without letting them know what they meant to me.

For letters I have actually sent, a mailbox icon (✉) appears next to the title in the table of contents and in the chapter. You can read more about my letter-writing journey in the appendix. I have also included questions for reflection for each chapter. I imagine you journaling about these questions or discussing them in a book club.

An old part of me is a little scared about writing all this to you and letting you read it, without knowing you. Can I trust you to see through my mistakes and shortcomings—to see my heart? Am I brave enough to tell the truth and not slant any stories to make myself look better or feel better? Here's what I know. I highly value extreme honesty. I've heard that the truth will set you free. This year, I have experienced that. I feel so much lighter now than when I began this journey.

So I invite you to explore my truths in these letters. I bless you on your journey through this book and through your life. Please take what serves you and hold it close. And release all that doesn't quite fit with a gentle breath of compassion.

In humble service and extreme hope,
Sarah

To Little Sarah, a Letter to Myself

I begin this book with a letter to myself. A therapist might call this my inner child. I believe one of the most important relationships we have is with ourselves, with all of our different inner voices. What then do I want to say to myself in order to feel that my relationship with myself is complete thus far? Mostly, I want myself to know how very much I love me.

Dear Self,

You are everything I could ever want in a daughter, a mother, a sister, or a friend. You are such a bright, strong light—shining in your own Sarah way, determined to light up the sky and every corner of the world. And you want others to play the "light up" game with you. "Tag, you're it! Turn the light on. Play with me."

You have a preciousness that is untarnishable, an innocence that remains pure and sweet. It's part of your core. You don't always feel this. You aren't always connected to it. Trust it. You can count on it. You can count on you.

Some in your life have a hard time with your exuberance and enthusiasm, your defiance of injustice, your anger at betrayal, or your hunger for intimacy. This is okay. Continue being the bright star that you are. Shine brightly, dear one. You will find others who shine alongside you. As Marianne Williamson wrote, "there is nothing enlightened about shrinking so that other people won't feel insecure around you."

You have just come across a most amazing piece of writing on Inner Independence. You have declared yours. Continue to live freely! Make decisions that feel good and right and true to you. Stay connected to Source. Stay connected to yourself, and you will automatically be hooked up with all the other connections (people, places, and things) you need and want. That's the kind of amazing world we live in.

I love you! I love that you now love yourself. I know it has sometimes seemed like a long and painful journey to this place. I am celebrating your arrival, your coming home to yourself.

I know there are still tender and hurt places within you. That doesn't make you broken or less than whole. Knowing about these parts and including them in your awareness with compassion makes you even more whole! It's another wonderful characteristic I love about you: your endless willingness to look inside and see what is there and take responsibility for it, for you.

I'm so proud of you for your contributions to this book. You have courage and strength and wisdom and love. And you are using your gifts in service of others. This is what you've always wanted: to have a purpose larger than your own selfish desires, to make a contribution that deeply touches the lives of others. You are my own role model! How cool is that?

With deep self-love and self-appreciation,

Me

To South Korea, Place of My Birth

I do not know much about my life before coming to the United States. The adoption agency has a record of my admittance to the Seoul City Baby Hospital. They assigned me a birthday based on an estimate of my age.

Growing up, I wasn't that interested in knowing about Korea. My adopted parents took me to gatherings with other adoptees. They asked if I'd like to go back to Korea someday. I didn't have a strong desire to go. Even when the Summer Olympics were held there in 1988, I was only mildly interested. It wasn't until I was involved in Soo Bahk Do, a South Korean martial art, that I returned to the land of my birth. I was thirty-four years old.

Dear South Korea,

You are the country of my birth, the home of my ancestors, and the place that handed me over to another people, another government, and another culture. I have so many feelings about you: gratitude, empathy, responsibility, and longing. I write to you today in the hopes of checking in with myself about how I feel about being so far away and so separated from the land of my birth.

I think of *Gone with the Wind* and Scarlett O'Hara's father saying, "Land, it's the only thing that matters; it's the only thing that lasts." I know there is some truth in that statement for me, about you, the land, my original land. And yet, when I visited you, I did not feel like I was coming home. I felt like a stranger, a somewhat frightened and wary stranger, in an unfamiliar place. I did not care for the way you smelled. I did not care for the food you offered me. But I did *love* the faces of your people, my people. I saw myself everywhere I looked—a very different experience from what I am used to, growing up and living in the north central Midwest region of the United States of America.

I want to thank you for your long history, for your rich culture, and for the challenges you've faced. Yours has not been an easy journey. You have been invaded time and time again. You and your people have been judged, repressed, and marginalized. And yet you still stand today. And some of the brightest, most successful and talented people come to the world from you.

Still, because of the way you were treated by some of the rest of the world, you could not take care of your children. Your people could not raise their own. And so you allowed adoptions by people in the United States of America. I was born sometime in the first half of 1971. I don't know much of my early story, only that somehow I was taken to the City Baby Hospital. I spent some time in your orphanage and then in foster care. When I was about nine months old, I was taken on a plane to Minnesota to meet my adoptive family. I used to think this was no big deal. I have no memories of the Korea of my infancy. And yet, when my son was nine months old, I realized how attached I must have been to the sights, smells, tastes, sounds, and textures of Korea—just like he was attached to his life.

I remember learning as a young girl that I could never be the president of the United States because I was a naturalized citizen and might have a bias towards Korea if America were ever at war with Korea. I couldn't ever deny this. Even though I didn't know anyone else from Korea, except for my adopted sister, I still felt a bond with the people there. Perhaps I knew that I might have relatives there.

I returned to you in the fall of 2005. I went as part of a martial arts group. I flew into Seoul and spent a day at the market and on a tour. I was scared of the people, the ones who thought I spoke the language because I looked like them. I remember thinking that I'd feel at home and love the atmosphere, the music, the food, etc. But I didn't. It didn't feel like home. I think I felt bad about that, like I was a traitor. I didn't fit there. And I don't really fit in America, either.

Regardless, I am glad that I came from you. I am also glad that I live somewhere else. Both feel true to me. And somehow, I feel okay holding these potentially conflicting thoughts. It's perfect that I was born in Korea. And it's perfect that I was raised by European-Lutherans. This dual heritage seems fitting for me—someone difficult to put in a box.

Thank you for giving me my roots and my wings—letting me live and letting me go live somewhere else.

With love and gratitude,
Sarah, one of your children

To My Birth Mother

I was adopted around the age of nine months. I came from South Korea. My adoptive parents were conscious about making adoption very matter of fact. They wanted a child; I was available. I remember my mom getting teary-eyed talking about my birth mother and how difficult it must have been for her to let go and trust. And so I grew up feeling like my adoption happened for a good reason and was a good thing. Even so, being torn from my biological family and my birth land at such a young age had an impact.

Over the years, I have written many letters to my birth mom. Some were filled with rage and hurt about feeling abandoned and unloved. Some were filled with longing and loneliness for a primary love I didn't feel I had experienced. Most were filled with questions. Now, at thirty-eight, I feel I have finally come to a true place of peace around my adoption, my relationship (or lack of one) with my biological family, and the questions surrounding my beginning.

This letter was written in preparation for my thirty-eighth birthday. I often write to my biological mom on my birthday or Christmas. But these letters have always been private. This time, I read my letter at the Joy Center, a beautiful retreat center in Ishpeming, Michigan, two days before my birthday. Then I read it again on Mother's Day at an ecumenical church service.

I was talking with a good friend in Norway about this book and this letter. He told me about an organization that recommends a method for dealing with grief. It was very similar to the process I followed with this letter. My friend believes that reading the letter out loud was an especially important part of this process. I do feel that this might be the last letter I write my biological mom, as it serves the purpose set out in this book: to complete the incomplete parts of that relationship. I can die at any moment and know that I am complete with this part of my life.

If you are a birth mother, adoptive mother, or adopted child, I send you a special blessing as you read this. May your own journey with adoption bring you peace.

Dear Mommy,

I have written you many letters over the years. Many of my early letters were filled with questions, seeking answers to why you left me. What was so unlovable about me? In the more recent past, my letters and thoughts to you have been about letting you know how very grateful I am that you gave me up for adoption. I recognize, now, that it must not have been an easy decision for you. I acknowledge and honor your place in my life now and forever.

This letter is about all of that. I'm almost thirty-eight years old now. Even writing that, I am reminded that every year, my birthday (or lack of an actual birthday) triggers thoughts about you. Some years, these thoughts created sadness or longing. Other years, these thoughts created wondering and curiosity. This year, these thoughts fill me with a deep love and a desire to connect to you, to let you know I turned out well and to put my mind at ease about how things turned out for you.

My adopted mom did a really good job of telling me what little she knew or could make up about you. I always believed you loved me and that you gave me up because you were scared that I was dying. I believe that you kept me for several weeks until I was so malnourished and sick that you feared for my life. Then you took me someplace where you could anonymously watch over me until the "right authorities" picked me up and took me to the City Baby Hospital in Seoul. I received the medical help I needed, including a blood transfusion and surgery for my head infection. By the time my adoptive parents received me at almost nine months of age, I was a round-faced, smiley, walking, talking toddler, full of curiosity and a willingness to attach myself quickly.

As a mother now myself, I can only imagine what it would have been like to watch my child get sick and not know what to do. As a little girl and young adult, I always thought that because I was a baby when all that happened, it didn't really matter. Then, at age twenty-four, I had my own son. And from the time I felt movement and saw his ultrasound photo, I was in love. And then, as he grew, sat up, talked, moved around, and bonded with me, I realized that I had probably bonded with both you and my foster mother (who carried me on her back). And that being an "infant" didn't mean that I wasn't affected by my early life experiences. This new insight gave me such compassion for myself and for you. I can't imagine having to give up my son after six weeks and never knowing what became of him.

So before writing anything more, I want you to know about me now. The life I experience is one full of blessings. The people in my life are good. I live on over eighty acres of land, relatively free of pollution. I spend a lot of time outside with my dog. Your grandson, Jonathon David, is healthy and beautiful and bright. He has deep, soulful eyes. He was born looking like a little old man. So I wonder if you've already seen what I'll look like as a little old lady.

I'm not sure what your spiritual beliefs might have been, but I believe in a Loving Source that created us and cares about us deeply. I hope you know this. I hope you know the peace that comes from believing and trusting in something greater than yourself. I think you must, in order to have given me up.

It's a little odd, but I never think of my biological father. I am a little curious, mostly for genetic reasons. But I think that either he didn't play a big role in my life (was gone before I was born) or somehow he was the reason you couldn't keep me, the reason your life was so difficult. And while I forgive him for that, I'm not interested in meeting him or really knowing him as a person. Although I would be open to that if he was. I'm not sure why I mention that to you. It might be important for you to know that it's you I've longed to know all these years.

And I do believe we will be reunited in some other life or in something like a heaven someday. And I don't want you to be afraid or worried about that. I have no bitterness or resentment towards you. Please release any guilt you have.

Why haven't I sought you out? I did try to find out more about my adoption and early life before visiting Korea, but I hit a dead end. And I think I haven't pursued it more because I feel complete about it. I feel cautious about putting too much effort into finding you, wanting you too much. I might feel like something is missing the rest of my earthly life without you if I decide I can't be happy without finding out about you. And right now, while I think about you and send loving thoughts towards you, because I haven't made it my goal to find you, I haven't felt disappointed that I haven't. Does that make any sense to you? I think if Jonathon were interested in his roots or needed genetic information, I would search for you, for his sake. And that doesn't seem fair, and I realize that in writing to you. But I include it anyway, because it's the truth. And I believe that the truth sets us free and all those around us.

Anyway, I love you, Mommy! I hope you are in heaven watching over Jonathon and me and smiling. That's where I picture you. I imagine that you are beautiful, gracious, and kind, with wise eyes and an easy smile. I imagine that you'd be proud of me and grateful to Nancy and Russ for raising me. And I bet you'd absolutely adore Jonathon. I wonder if he would remind you of my brother or father or your father. There's passion and spirit in our family line, I can tell you that! And so much courage (that I can tell from you) and so very much love.

Thank you, Mommy, for making the difficult decision you made. It has made all the difference in my life. Please free your heart of any worries or guilt or doubt.

Till we meet in the flesh or the spirit,
Your loving and grateful daughter,
Park Chung Ja

To the First Home I Remember

The first home I remember was the house where I grew up. I have many memories of that house and my time spent there. I realized while writing this letter that I was not only writing to my home. I was also writing to my parents and to my childhood. I had a happy childhood! And this home was a big part of that. It feels important to remember the positive. For so long, my childhood memories have mostly included hurts and wrongdoings. I loved walking, room by room, in my mind, uncovering rich, sweet moments from my youth. This is extreme honesty, too. When I have a one-sided belief about something, it helps me to look for the other side, a more expansive truth.

Dear First Home,

I loved you soooo much! I grew up surrounded by your walls. You witnessed most of the first twelve years of my life.

I could draw the building plans for you in my mind, placing walls, appliances, and people in their appropriate places. It's been so long since I've seen you, and yet I walk through you in my mind often.

You witnessed such a transformative part of my life. You saw me grow from toddler to pre-teen.

I inhabited two of your rooms as bedrooms. When I was in third grade, we remodeled. My first room was my very own room, and this was important to me. It was the first room on the right as you came down the hallway from the living room. Looking in from the door, my bed was in the right-hand corner. My closet was along the left. I had a nightstand by my bed and a toy shelf at the end of my bed. Most of the time, there was a sheepskin rug on the floor next to the bed. I lay sprawled out on my belly there, reading books, talking to stuffed animals, and cutting out paper dolls.

My closet was big, and I sat inside it and cried when I didn't want anyone to see or hear my hurt. But you saw. You witnessed. Your walls kept my secrets.

In the basement, we had a large play area. My little wooden kitchen set was there, along with my old-fashioned school desk and chalkboard for educating my stuffed animals and occasionally my sister and her dolls.

We had a large cardboard box filled with a most amazing collection of dress-up clothes. It included bridesmaid dresses from our favorite aunt, dance recital costumes from our older cousin, an old fur coat from our great grandmother, a wig, high-heeled shoes, purses, clunky costume jewelry, and hats. We had old tattered blankets for shawls as well. I must have transformed myself a thousand times throughout my childhood— from queen to film star, mom to ice skater, dancer to soap opera character, nightclub singer, waitress, teacher, and more. We put on shows with made-up songs and Broadway numbers. We made up dances as well. None of us were in dance or were taking voice lessons at the time, but we were enthusiastic and confident.

I learned to climb trees in my own backyard. We had a tall maple tree that rained "helicopters" on us as we played in the sandbox. When my boy cousins came for a visit, they both leaped into the branches and scooted nimbly up the tree, into the very top. We could hardly see them. I hadn't even sat in the lowest branch, though I had hung upside down from it. Today I have a moderate fear of heights. But back then I just wanted to impress my cousins and not be left out of any fun. So I carefully scooted up the tree as well. The most frightening part was coming back down, where I had to look to see where I was stepping and was forced to realize how high up I was and how far down I could fall.

We'd play for hours in our sandbox, in the shade of your porch walls. We would "cook" for long periods of time: mixing and stirring, patting and folding, baking in the hot sun, decorating with leaves, buds, flowers, and grass. Occasionally we'd build a city or drive our brother's trucks or car around.

Our backyard bordered a tree nursery. We learned how to cross-country ski there. One time, the neighbor girl and I were playing out there in the rain. She got stuck in the mud. I had to run and get my mom. She pulled my friend out, leaving her boot. My friend was screaming and crying. I thought it was kind of funny. I bet you did, too.

For a long time, there were empty lots at the end of our road. We built forts in the weeds and in the trees. I scraped my side on a rusty nail and thought I might have lockjaw (I had just learned about it in health class). I made my mom show me my tetanus shot records (being a doctor's kid, I probably wasn't in a lot of danger of being under-immunized). We used the spare lot to set up obstacle courses for "Olympics" or jumps for biking. Later, someone developed that whole area, building what my dad called "chicken-coop condos." We had a swing set on the side of our house. In the summer, we'd put our kiddie pool at the base of the slide. Iowa summers in the 1970s would get from the mid-eighties to over a hundred degrees. We stayed cool by eating Popsicles, drinking Kool-Aid, and splashing in our pool. One day, the two neighbor girls, my sister, and I were swimming and playing in the water. When we were done, we took off our wet swim-suits and hung them on the jungle gym, then continued playing outside. A plumber or some other service man came over to fix something. He told my mom, "Lady, there are naked girls running around in your yard." It was time to go inside.

You, house, were on a hill. Our concrete, one-car driveway was very steep. We loved it. We played CHiPs (California Highway Patrol), based on a TV show, with the other neighborhood kids. We were all on bikes. Our favorite part was getting "the call" and being sent out on a "mission." We all started at the top of the driveway and went shooting down the street to the scene of a "crime." When we got roller skates (the metal kind that attach to your shoes), we dared each other to go down the driveway. Neither my sister nor I would start at the top and make it all the way down. We'd run off into the grass or start part way up. My girlfriend (with boot skates and pompoms on the laces) was the first to take the dare. She made it look easy. I tried, too, and was successful. My dad saw us, said no, and that was the end of that.

When we built the addition onto the back of our house, we had a skating rink in the new foundation. We roller-skated around in our personal rink for what seemed like a long time but was probably only a few weeks. My bedroom became my parents' room. Actually, it became their master closet. And I moved into my sister's room. I occupied the back half. We roomed together for three years. Although she was the tidier of the two of us, I still missed my privacy. This is when I overcame my extreme fear of our basement. I still didn't like it. But I braved the cold, the silverfish, and the potential dark for solace. I hid under the Ping-Pong table, at the back of the large playroom area. There were old carpets and padding stored here, making a cushy, if bumpy, surface for lying on. I'd read books and nap with my stuffed dog, Le Mutt (who looked a lot like my current best canine friend and mutt, Strider). Sometimes I'd write in my diary. Sometimes I'd shed a few tears.

Although I was excited to move, I also hated leaving you, my home. You knew all my special places. I promised you I'd return. I think I even promised that I'd come back and buy you when I was an adult. I did go back once to see you. It had only been a year or two since our move. The new owners had changed your appearance by painting you (blue, I think) and adding tacky, white, fake shutters. They also built a storage shed in the yard, where our garden used to be. You no longer looked like my house. I turned my eyes (and my heart) away from you. It's better to not like something than like it and miss it and hurt because it's changed. I didn't really mourn the loss. I didn't really say a final farewell to you, or my childhood town, or my own youth.

I hope to go back and visit you again. I'd love to walk my old route to school. I'd like to climb your maple tree again or at least sit in its shade and write a letter.

I realize this letter is to more than just you. I'm writing to myself, too, to remind myself of my happy childhood. The '70s were a great time to be me—to be a kid. I had so much freedom, so few responsibilities. I came from a good family, not having to worry about poverty, abuse, or neglect. I am so grateful for my upbringing, so grateful for the days spent in your shelter.

Love,
Sarah—one of the children who occupied you for a time

To Molly, My Sister

My early relationship with my sister was one of competition, jealousy, and resentment. Today our relationship is full of love, respect, and mutual support and encouragement. This letter tells the story of my inner struggles in our relationship and how I came to understand her point of view.

I sent her this letter for her thirty-sixth birthday this year. I also read this letter at the Joy Center in honor of my dear sister.

Dear Molly,

Oh my sister, my beloved sister. How I hated you when you came into my life! How I envied you and resented you during our childhood. How far apart we grew during much of our early adulthood. And now, how very appreciative I am for our sisterhood, for you being a role model of healthy boundaries and truth telling. I am so grateful for you in my life, so sorry for all the years I wasted not liking you, and so very hopeful for the rest of our lives together.

They say that how people treat us and what they think of us says more about them than it does about us. I completely agree. My disliking you was all about me. It was about me being three years old when you came. I was just getting into the groove with Mom and Dad, trusting that I wouldn't be left or uprooted again. I was happy. I got all the attention. They adored me, and I adored them right back. I'm sure there was some preparation involved when we were expecting you. Perhaps they told me you were coming or I was going to be a big sister. I have no memories of that. In fact, I have only a very vague memory of my life without you.

I do not remember your arrival either. Although later, I do remember being told about it over and over when we were young. I remember feeling somewhat proud of my naughty three-year-old self who asked to hold you and then clawed you across the face. I felt affirmed in hearing that story. "Yep, I knew from the beginning that she was the enemy." Something deep within me sensed that you were a threat. You could take away everything I loved and needed in this world. And maybe because I thought you could, I experienced that.

I remember being told that I had to be quiet and not wake the baby. I remember being told I was too big to play with the baby. I was too rough, too. And too loud. And too rambunctious. And too old for little kid chairs and toys. I went from being Mom and Dad's perfect little ray of sunshine to the thing most troubling in their life—or at least a potential trigger for one of your tantrums or nightmares.

I remember your howling. I remember waking up and hearing you wailing. I went down the hall to see what was wrong. "Get back to bed," I was told by our stressed-out parents. I lay in bed feeling sad, left out, not knowing what was going on, not being allowed to find out.

I remember the look on Mom's face when she watched you play at the playground or swim in the pool. She adored you. She said over and over how pretty you were. She bounced you on her lap (the one I was now too big to sit on). I thought maybe Dad wouldn't like you because you were so naughty (fussy and crying and defiant), but he seemed very patient with you. I kept waiting for them to see in you what I saw, a "bad" little baby ruining the good life we once shared. But they never saw that. They loved you so much.

And for some reason, I couldn't fathom that they could love us both. Because the amount of attention I received was less than the amount of attention you received, I decided they chose you to replace me. I thought that I must have done something very bad or they found out something was wrong with me and decided to put all their hopes and dreams into a new adopted baby girl.

I hated you for this. Until I was a teenager, I didn't think about our parent's behavior and any role they played in our sibling animosity. I only thought that if you weren't my sister, I'd have all the love and attention.

There were a few moments growing up when we were connected because it was us versus them, like when the bullies followed us to school and picked on us. But mostly it felt like war between us.

I had no idea that you didn't realize how I felt and why until we went to the Bahamas together and you shared how hurt you were by something mean I did to you when we moved. You couldn't fathom why I would have done something like that. I tried to explain, but could really only apologize.

There was nothing at all wrong with you, Molly. And now that we are adults, we've actually become friends. You have been very generous to me, my son, and both of my husbands. You seem to have completely forgiven me for all my cruelties in our youth. Once in awhile, when we're both home, I feel like we compete a bit for Mom and Dad's attention. But mostly, it seems like we have grown to respect and love one another.

You are bright, beautiful, healthy, creative, and loving. You deserve good friends and family and work. I want us to stay connected throughout the rest of our lives. Thank you for your generous spirit as I worked through my jealousy all these years.

I love you.

Your big sister,
Sarah

To Chad, My First Love

I remember him so well! He lived down the street. We spent a lot of time together, along with several other boys and a few girls in our neighborhood. We were in the same class through fourth grade.

When I moved away, we lost touch. But he will always have a special place in my heart. Until now, I haven't ever tried to find him.

Dearest Chad,

Oh how I have loved you! From the time I was a little girl (my mom says we rolled down the hill in our diapers together) I have loved you. You were my best friend, my playmate, and my first crush. I adored you!

I remember being at your house in a huge empty room with wood floors listening to Elvis (I didn't even know who Elvis was) while you danced and lip-synched to the music. I was probably as much of an adoring fan of yours as any Elvis ever had.

I remember how mad you were when you found out those boys were bullying me on the way to school. I remember you plotted to beat up the younger brother once his older brother was out of the picture. It felt so good to have someone who wanted to right the wrong I felt was being done to me. You were my knight in shining armor.

I remember when you told me how to make babies and I heard the "f" word for the first time. Intuitively, I knew what it meant.

I remember when I moved away to Wisconsin, I worried that you'd forget about me. And when I came back to visit after being gone a year, you were so smitten with someone else that it stung. So I pretended to have a boyfriend back home to cover up my hurt. I tried to make myself stop caring about you or thinking of you. But I never really did.

I know your full name. And I remember you had a birthday in the fall, maybe September. And I can still see your boyish eyes (green perhaps) from behind a lock of sandy brown hair. You were so full of life.

Once, when I got one of those ads for "find your old boyfriend" or something like that on the computer, I typed in your name. But I was too afraid of what I'd find. And I deleted it before the search began.

My heart is still so full of love for you, Chad. I hope your life has been good. I hope you are healthy and happy. I hope you have a little boy who brings you as much joy as you brought to me. And I hope you remember me, too—and know how very much I loved you.

I think some day I'll have the courage to look you up, to face whatever there is to face. It's not like I believe we should be together as a couple. It's just that you are such a prominent figure from my childhood, it's strange to have lost track of you.

Something in me worries that things didn't turn out okay for you and that somehow if we had stayed connected, I could have been the touchstone you needed. How egocentric is that! And yet it's what I think sometimes when I think of you.

So it's time I free myself from the fear of being rejected or of discovering something sad. I'm going to find you and send you this letter. If we should meet again, I'll tell you how much I have loved you and love you still. Till then, I wish all the best for you!

I love you, Chad Jeremy Coffin.

—Sarah

To the Cedar Falls Bullies

For about a year, my sister and I were bullied as we walked to school each morning. The bullies were two neighbor boys. One was a few years older than I was, and the other was younger than I was but older than my sister. They didn't beat us up, thankfully. But they called us names, including racial slurs, threw worms at us, and pulled off our hats or mittens and filled them with snow. They'd stand close behind us making weird sounds. They'd block our path so we had to go around them on the grass, and then they'd block our path again. We came to dread our walks to school. But we never talked about it or told our parents. I told another neighbor boy that I hated them. He said he did, too, and that sometime when the older boy wasn't around, he was going to beat up the younger boy. I don't remember that ever happening. But I know I wished them both dead. Later in my life, I was the bully to a girl at a day care when I was a child and to my first dog when I was a young adult. I don't really understand why I bullied others. Perhaps I felt jealousy or impatience. Certainly I did not feel good about it or myself. I think the same must be true about those boys.

Dear Cedar Falls Bullies,

I'm sorry I don't remember your names. For so long, I tried not to think about you. Then, you were just "the bullies." Now I think of you as real people. I think of you both as the little boys from back then and as grown men now. And I want you to know that I forgive you. Maybe you never think about that time. Maybe my sister and I belong to a large group of people one or both of you has bullied. Perhaps as a teen I watched too many after-school specials about dysfunction in America. Maybe it is only in my over-active imagination that you came from a troubled home. I didn't know you well enough to even remember your names.

All I knew about you then, and all I really remember now, is that you seemed to take great pleasure in terrorizing my sister and me on our way to school. Although we tried our best not to give you a show, you seemed determined to see us scream or cry or run. We did not do any of these things. Heads held high, we continued walking no matter what. Getting to school safely, with pride, was our goal, and we would not be stopped. This was probably our coping mechanism. We couldn't control how you treated us, but we could control our response. I wonder what you thought about this. I'm sure you sensed our fear anyway—saw us walk faster or look behind us to see if you were coming.

None of that matters now. What I'm curious about is you. What happened to make you that way? Why would you work so hard to elicit a fear response in other children, girls? You spoke cruel, hate-filled words. You threatened violence. We witnessed you beating up a boy. What thoughts were going through your heads during that time?

My theory now is that you either were bullied at home by a parent or older sibling or witnessed it happening to someone else in your family. I have always felt sorry for the victim in a story or situation. I've quickly judged the perpetrator as bad, wrong, mean, or sick. But perpetrators aren't born like that. People don't start out filled with hate, wanting to hurt others. Something must have happened to you.

I hope you have turned your lives around. I hope you are not abusing your spouses or children or coworkers. I hope that you have peace in your hearts, that you've forgiven whatever and whomever from your past, and that you've forgiven yourselves as well.

Blessings of peace to you,
Sarah

✒ To Martha, My First Music Teacher

Martha was my first and probably the best private music teacher I had. She was patient, kind, gifted, creative, and fun. I didn't recognize most of this when I had her as a teacher. Music lessons were frustrating for me. I wanted to be good immediately. I didn't want my collarbone to hurt or my fingers to sting. I wanted to be able to play songs I heard on the radio. I didn't understand why posture and technique were so important.

Besides teaching me how to play the violin, Martha exposed me to a variety of music, including folk, classical, jazz, and country. She taught me basic music theory and instilled in me a love for good music. Music continues to inspire me and feed my soul. While I don't make music on my own anymore, I appreciate it and others who do.

I'm thankful that my parents chose Martha as my teacher. She is more than just a fine musician and teacher; she is an outstanding human being.

Dear Martha,

I am so happy that we are back in touch (since Christmas 2008). I know we've had a few letters and birthday and Christmas cards over the years, and I have really appreciated that. I've been writing letters recently to a lot of people from my past. Part of the purpose has been for me to remember and acknowledge the people who helped me. Another part has been to complete any "old business" that has me feeling bad about myself or another person.

I believe I wrote you a letter similar to this several years ago, but I just want to say this again. I know I was not the most pleasant or cooperative violin student or girl when I knew you. In fact, I'd say I was pretty rude and bratty sometimes. I remember complaining and refusing to play at lessons. I remember my mom saying I'd been rude to you and that my disrespectful behavior was really embarrassing. Yet what I remember about you is that you were this steady beacon of light, ready and willing to teach me, show me things, and encourage me. I don't ever remember you being mean to me or strict. I don't remember ever being afraid of you. And now, as an adult, I have such deep, deep gratitude for my appreciation of music and the foundation you laid in my heart and my soul for a lifelong love of classical music and string instruments in particular.

I love the cello and the viola especially. And I remember you played the viola in the symphony. We came to at least one of your concerts. I remember thinking, "Oh, she's more than just my teacher." What a full life you have lived! What huge contributions you have made.

Most of all, I want you to know that when I am asked to name an adult or teacher from my childhood that believed in me and made a difference in my life, I think of you. You were such an integral part of my youth. And I took you for granted and was even mean to you!

I am sorry, Martha. Please forgive the rude little girl I was and see the woman I have become. I know you already do. When I started writing to you, you responded with grace and love and compassion.

It's one of my dreams to visit the town of my childhood again. And when I do, I'd love to go to church with you and take you out for brunch afterwards as a small token of my appreciation for your presence in my life.

I love you!

With deep gratitude,
Sarah

✒ To My Aunt Heidi, Role Model of Forgiveness

My aunt Heidi was in my life for about ten years. She was my mom's brother's third wife. She made a huge impact on me. The older I get, the more I recognize the grace and love she epitomized in my youth. Though we have lost touch, I am forever grateful for her gift of forgiveness.

Dear Heidi,

Hello! It's been so, so long since I've had any kind of communication with you. My last memories of you are when Emily was a baby. Now she's a young woman graduated from college.

I am writing to tell you that other than my son, you are the person I have learned the most from about forgiveness. You set an example with me when I was just a teen that I have not forgotten. And now I am in a similar situation with my husband's children. I remember your example, and it gives me hope for our family. I want to be as loving in my situation as you were with me.

I first heard about you when I lived in Iowa, when I was younger than twelve years old. I remember my mom doing laundry in the basement and telling me that her brother was getting a divorce (from his second wife) because he'd had an affair with his boss's daughter (you). I'm not sure how much of that I understood, but I knew that my mom was upset because she was crying and could barely talk about it. I'm not sure why she was talking about it with me or if I was just overhearing her on the phone with someone else. But I knew that she didn't think highly of you. Therefore I wasn't going to, either.

I remember the first time I met you, at Grandma and Grandpa's. We all went out for dinner. You were so incredibly beautiful and kind and interesting. I could see you winning over my grandparents and my aunts and my sister. But I was determined to be loyal to my mom and not like you. I gave you dirty looks across the table, certain they would crush you or anger you so you would lash out at me and everyone would see what a horrible person you were. But none of that happened. You didn't give me dirty looks back, nor did you get angry at me. You did try to talk with me a bit, and then just focused on my sister after receiving either curt answers or a cold shoulder.

Gradually, you were accepted into our family. Even my mom talked with you, and my aunts both adored you. I came around as well. But I always felt a bit embarrassed about the way I had acted. You never treated me differently than my sister or made me feel bad. You didn't tell my mom or anyone else how I had behaved.

One night, when we were together at my grandparents' home, I was watching your girls in the bath while the adults were visiting after dinner. I remember you came in to check on them. It was then that I got up my courage to apologize for the way I had treated you. I was probably somewhere between fourteen and sixteen years old. I will never forget the sweet, appreciative, and loving look in your eyes and the serenity in your face when you said something like, "Don't give it a second thought. It was a difficult situation. I completely understand." Although I knew you wouldn't yell at me or anything, I was still blown away by your answer. You recognized it was just the circumstances, nothing personal. And when I could see past the circumstance and get to know you as a person, it'd be fine, or it wouldn't, but that it really wasn't about you.

Now I find myself as the one who is resented and disliked by my husband's children. In my heart, I know that a lot of it is just the circumstances, like with you. But I have not been nearly as gracious, understanding, or forgiving. I have wanted an apology. I have felt personally wronged and rejected. I sometimes feel very angry about the whole situation. This is all craziness! I think of you and remind myself that Aunt Heidi would not act like this!

Thank you for your fine example.

I hope your life has turned out well for you. You are such a kind, intelligent, beautiful, and sincere woman.

Love,
Your niece Sarah

To the People of Greenwood

My family moved the summer between my sixth and seventh grades. I was filled with hopes and dreams. Within months, I was heartbroken. The remainder of my time in Greenwood was a roller-coaster ride of highs and lows. I see now it was typical, in many ways, of most teenagers' experiences. Then, I blamed the city and the people for the lows. I saw this place as different from the "real world." I didn't see my part in creating my experience there. Now I do.

Dear People of Greenwood,

I came to you with such hopes and dreams. You represented a clean slate, a new start. I could reinvent myself. I could be popular. And I wanted that very much. When I left Cedar Falls, I could already see, by sixth grade, that I was not going to be one of the "cool" people. I didn't wear name-brand clothes. I didn't have blond hair or blue eyes. I thought that in a new town, a country town, I could become fashionable and pretty and popular.

And so I came to you wanting to belong. I worked so hard to fit in with you—wear what you were wearing, like the boys you thought were cool, and be the kind of person that would impress you. I would have said or done anything to make you like me. But you didn't. Maybe you could see how much I wanted your attention, and that repulsed you. Maybe you sensed the power you had over me and used that to make me pay for every other new kid who came along and made you feel backwards.

In that first year of school, all the girls in my class but two and several of the girls in the eighth grade class sent me a letter they had all signed telling me to move back where I came from. This was a low point in my life. There were other painful moments as well. But that's not actually what I wanted to say. There have been other letters I've written to you, as a whole, or certain individuals—letters I never sent—the kind you learn how to write in therapy to get your angry, hurt feelings out on paper. But that isn't the purpose of this letter.

The reason I am writing this and including it in this book is to let you know (and to highlight for my readers) that I now see my part in all this. And that has been the missing step in reclaiming my "victim" self from my teenage experience and reempowering her. I now see that no matter how I felt on the inside, I was projecting a facade of aloofness on the outside. I wanted you to think I was cool. You thought I was heartless. I thought it'd make you like me. Instead, you wanted to break my spirit. I see how being untrue to myself and putting on airs created tension between us.

And I was mean to many of you as well. In my heart, I secretly wished bad things for some of you. When I would hear stories about your families—stories of parents pouring boiling water on the children, stories of parents not coming to special events, stories of drug use and ridicule—I didn't care. I only cared about me and my unpopularity. I feel ashamed to admit that I didn't see you as people, only as potential stepping stones towards what I wanted or road blocks to the same.

Years after I graduated and moved away, I held the belief that one day I would come back and "show you." I had a strong desire to prove my worthiness and your unworthiness. "See? Look who's got the most friends now (I didn't actually develop meaningful friendships until the mid-90s)! Look who's making money (I actually wasn't). Look who's still thin and pretty (like that's what matters)."

I won't lie. I still fantasize sometimes about attending a reunion or coming home for the holidays and meeting some of you and hearing the praises and receiving the attention I longed for as a teen. But that isn't what really matters to me. I recognize that longing as my ego seeking a (false) sense of belonging. What's most important to me now is letting you know that I'm sorry for anything I did or said during those years that made you feel bad about yourselves. It may have been accidental, in my intense focus on myself. It may have been on purpose: out of revenge or just feeling relieved that I wasn't the one being picked on. I joined in on cruel behavior towards others.

I share my story in the hopes that you and other readers will see past people's behavior to their hearts. What makes a girl so cruel? What makes someone appear so stuck up? Why would someone pretend to have boyfriends? Perhaps all that outer behavior—clothes, academic achievement, extracurricular activities—are attempts at belonging, seeking recognition and approval.

You would think that after my experience, I'd be extra-sensitive to others' pain at not belonging. I haven't been. I've been so grateful to fit and belong in different groups that I have often been either oblivious to or unconcerned about the feelings of those on the outside. I'm not proud of this. And I don't quite understand it. I am hoping that, by writing this letter, I am shining the light of awareness on this part of me so that I can no longer act this way in secret (from myself).

To the people of Greenwood and people everywhere, I have a request. When behaviors seem hurtful, bizarre, or conceited, please look past all that to the heart of the person. See what they might be craving in this situation. Speak to and be with them as a person who has a social need they're wanting filled. I don't think I'm alone. I think every single one of us has hurt places that at times we try to cover and hide. And that our "hiding" sometimes looks and feels very odd, distancing, or hurtful to others. That's not always our intention. And we don't always notice the consequences because we're too wrapped up in our own pain and struggle.

What would it be like if we shed the facades and met one another heart to heart?

With apologies, respect, and hope,
Sarah

To Mr. Navrestad, My Band Director

Mr. Navrestad was one of my favorite teachers. He gave me clarinet lessons and directed the junior high and high school concert band, pep band, and marching band. He was also the father of one of my classmates. When I was an adult, he was diagnosed with Lou Gehrig's disease. My parents went to the same church he and his wife attended. My mom would update me on his condition and later on the funeral arrangements. During that time, I thought a lot about writing him a letter. I never did.

I wish I would have had the courage to write this sooner, to visit him, and to reach out to his family. What is it that keeps me from following my heart sometimes?

Note: I sent this letter to his widow.

Dear Mr. Navrestad,

Hello! It's been about half my life ago since I last wrote to you. Now you're dead. But here I am, writing to you again. I was home, in Greenwood, for Easter. I saw your wife playing the organ during church. I felt the old twinge of guilt I feel whenever I see her. This letter is long overdue.

You were one of my very favorite teachers! You were always kind to me. I know that I did not play the clarinet beautifully. I'm sure you, as my band director, knew that from the time you first heard me play. But you called me a diamond in the rough. You worked with me, offered me duets for competition, and eventually moved me to the bass clarinet.

Yes, you spit when you talked, and we all laughed about it in junior high. By the time we graduated, however, none of us cared. We loved you. We loved the way you encouraged Scott to learn many different instruments and compose his own piece for our band to play. We loved the way you beamed with pride at us when we won awards at competitions.

And I was one of those youth who didn't always remember my instrument or my music. My reeds were sometimes cracked. And you, though clearly disappointed and often irritated with me, were always supportive, coming to my rescue.

After I graduated from high school, I wrote to you from college for awhile. I remember mailing you a pen or pencil that said "uff da" on it. You used to say that a lot hearing me play.

I remember thinking about you when I watched *Mr. Holland's Opus.* Even then I wanted to write you a letter to tell you how much you meant to me. I remember thinking about you a lot when I found out you were diagnosed with Lou Gehrig's disease. It was after I read *Tuesdays with Morrie*, and I remember thinking that the relationship between the author and Morrie was somewhat similar to ours. I always felt like I was special to you in some way.

But I didn't write to you either of those times. And I didn't attend your funeral. And I don't think I've ever expressed my condolences to your family, even though I've seen your wife and your daughter, Laura, since your death.

This troubles me. Oh, I don't think you really minded. You probably knew my shy and awkward teenage self, though posing as a confident young woman, would not have been able to handle death and dying and meaningful conversation. Still, I knew I should go see you before you died. And yet I allowed whatever was happening in my life and my lack of courage (although I didn't admit that part) to excuse me from visiting you.

I'm sorry, Mr. Navrestad! I loved you! I am so grateful for your nurturing, attentiveness, mentoring, musical training, and love during those very difficult times. You are one of my heroes.

I know you can hear me and see me now. I don't play my clarinet anymore, but I imagine I'll receive my mom's instruments when she no longer plays. I just might be in a community band someday, smiling as I think of my mother and you!

With apologies and love,
Sarah

To St. Olaf College

St. Olaf College is a small liberal arts college located in Northfield, Minnesota. It is a beautiful campus. A lot of Norwegian Lutherans attend this school. It is well-known for its music program.

I attended St. Olaf, my parents' alma mater, for a year and a half before transferring to the College of St. Catherine, where I received my BA. Although I did not think St. Olaf was a fit at the time, I regret transferring schools. I remain an "Ole" at heart.

Dear St. Olaf College,

During my senior year of high school, I was so proud to be selected for early admission. I felt at home when I visited your campus. I loved the idea of being a college student, of being an "Ole." I even practiced the "Um! Yah! Yah!" fight song so I would know it when I attended football games—though I never went. I imagined myself as the typical student: attending daily chapel, taking a full course load, studying, dating, singing in the choir, and enjoying campus life.

After graduating from high school, however, I spent the summer at a Christian camp near Rochester, Minnesota, where I met my first husband. I was eighteen. He was twenty-six. I hadn't learned how to say no and be okay with hurting someone's feelings.

By the time I came to you as a first-year student, I had already been proposed to several times. I wasn't going to have the "common" college experience unless I broke up with my boyfriend. Though I tried a few times, I couldn't do it when he threatened suicide.

And so I rarely went to chapel. I didn't sing in the choir, although I took voice lessons. I dropped classes so I could hang out with him and work. I didn't date anyone else. And I didn't really enjoy campus life. I didn't get along that well with my roommate. I didn't really make a lot of other friends.

But now, at almost forty, I think back on that time with great appreciation. Even though I didn't choose to get as much out of that experience as I could have (my dad was willing to pay for me to spend a month in London studying theatre), I still have good memories.

I remember some of the fabulous teachers. I had a high school math teacher, who was on sabbatical from her high school job, for calculus. She was awesome. I remember thinking that if I could have her for every class, I could be a math major. I was in the paracollege, so a lot of my classes were team-taught and interdisciplinary. I loved the English-religion class that was required. We read some amazing novels, and I probably wrote one of the best papers I've ever written. I thought about things in new ways and heard interesting opinions from my classmates as well.

I love that you're an honor-system campus. We could leave our purses, backpacks, anything on the floor outside the lunchroom. We took tests using the honor system. At the end, we signed our name that we hadn't cheated or witnessed anyone else cheating.

One thing I think I found a bit troubling was that there was a lot of drinking on a "dry" campus. I lived on a floor with about twenty-four other women. At the end of the weekend, the recycling bins would be overflowing with beer cans. The men's floors were worse. It obviously was *not* a dry campus. When I was complaining about this to a friend whose son graduated from you, she told me that she felt okay about the drinking because at least no one was driving anywhere, as most students do not have cars on campus. At first I resisted this idea with my lofty ideals of "walk your talk." Now I see how this fits with who you are, both idealistic and accepting.

Since I left your beautiful campus, I have gone through many stages: thinking private schools are full of rich snobs, wishing I was more of a rich snob myself, feeling like college was a waste because I really didn't "do" anything with my degree, and now being so thankful for my liberal arts foundation. I've thought I wanted to be an expert at something. I can see that those people, the MDs and PhDs, are the ones our society honors as having wisdom. I wanted to have wisdom (or at least be seen as having wisdom). Now I realize I have something that is just as valuable. I have breadth of knowledge. I have been exposed to a moderate amount of lots of things. It has given me an appreciation for and a comfort with many different kinds of people, situations, and ways of knowing. I know that I can learn almost anything, including calculus and how to play basic chords on a guitar. I know that different people have different passions and interests and talents. I believe that a lot of this knowing came from you: your faculty and staff, your students, and your alumni (two of whom raised me).

Thank you, St. Olaf College. I hope to return to your campus someday and graduate as an "Ole."

With appreciation,
Sarah

To Pinstripes Petites

I began working at Pinstripes Petites as a sales associate the summer between my first and second years at St. Olaf College. I loved the world of fashion. I loved the clothes. I loved the people—at first. Then things took a sour turn. I became one of the stereotypical disgruntled employees, feeling underpaid, overworked, and unappreciated.

One day I bought a bunch of clothing I knew a department store was carrying. I purchased it with my employee discount and then had my fiancé return it at the department store for full price. As if that wasn't bad enough, when I came to work the next day, I noticed we had extra stock of the items I'd purchased. So I bagged them up as if they were my purchases from the day before and returned them again. That was stealing. No one ever noticed. I never confessed. A few months after that, I received a better job offer and gave my notice.

Dear Pinstripes Petites,

I stole money from you by returning items I hadn't purchased. It was wrong. I remember listening to tapes about the "shadow side" around five years ago. They talked about making amends for situations that still held power over you. I remember thinking about this incident. I remember that the example on the tapes was even similar to mine. But I did not seek you out to make amends. I was worried about going to jail when I had a young son. I was worried about embarrassment and shame. I'm still worried about those things. But I'm willing to risk those to come clean because it has never felt okay to me that I did this.

Sure, I justified it, like everyone else who has stolen. "The company owed me. Other people were probably doing it, too." The Arbinger Institute defines "justification" as the act of making something crooked straight (I'm paraphrasing). You don't have to justify, explain, or apologize when you're straight and pure and in integrity with yourself.

In any case, I am sorry that I was not a trustworthy employee. I am sorry that I might have contributed to your company not being financially successful. I am sorry that I stole from you. I am enclosing a check for $250. I believe the outfit included a skirt, jacket, and knit top. The retail value would have been more. The cost would have been less. It was in 1991.

With apology,
Sarah

To Me on the Day of My First Wedding

I thought about letters I could write to my ex-husband. However, to really feel at peace with this time in my life, I needed to write a letter to the part of me that chose to marry Skip—to that small young bride who both doubted and trusted so deeply. I have so much love and compassion for my barely twenty-year-old self. I think somehow the me of today was present at that wedding, shaking her head with thoughts of the pain to come *and* smiling with love about the baby to be born and the lessons to be learned.

Dear Sarah, on the day of your first wedding,

Oh my little sweetheart! I see you getting ready, wanting to be beautiful and wanting to be saved. I see the doubt in your heart and hear your intuition screaming that you don't want to marry this man. I hear you pleading silently with your father as you prepare to walk down the aisle, "Ask me if I really want to do this." I feel your courage, preparing to tell him the truth, "No." And I see your resolve and maturity in holding your head high, walking down that aisle, and sincerely pledging your life and your love to someone you don't believe is really meant for you.

Oh Sarah, my sweet, twenty years, one month, and one-week-old self. I have such great compassion for you. If I were there, I would have whispered in your ear, "It's okay. It's all going to turn out just fine. It's okay if you marry him: you'll have the most amazing child together, you'll model compassionate co-parenting with an ex-spouse, and you'll meet someone else." I would have told you how beautiful you were, and that you didn't have to starve yourself to like yourself. I would have told you that composure and poise are fine traits, but vulnerability, transparency, intimacy, and authenticity are much better qualities for long-term, trusting relationships.

I love that you knew your truth and were willing to tell it to yourself on that day. I love that you were prepared to share your secret if anyone asked. I want you to know that who you are today is someone who shares her truth when she needs to, whether anyone asks for it or not (even when they might not appreciate hearing it in that moment).

Who you are today is someone who can feel equally beautiful in a second-hand gown from Goodwill or a Jessica McClintock wedding gown. Who you are today is someone whose twenty-year-old self would think was chubby but who has a much better relationship with her body and herself than ever before. Who you are today is someone who might still feel awkward crying in front of people but who knows that it's real and there's nothing to be embarrassed about. Who you are today is someone who occasionally veers toward the martyr's path but is aware of this tendency and catches it much sooner than in the past. Who you are today believes she is lovable, loving, and loved by the people closest to her. Who you are today has many true friends, people who see your essence and cherish their relationships with you, people who give wise counsel when you are in need.

I am you, and you are me. And there is one of us who is fifty and sixty and more. In one sense, we are all we have—all we can really ever count on.

Know that I am with you. And I carry you with me. And I love you! And we're going to be just fine.

With self-love,
Sarah

To Margie and Bill, My Ex-Parents-in-Law

I was married to my first husband a month and a week after I turned twenty. We separated a few months before I turned twenty-seven. We divorced when I was thirty. During our marriage, I didn't know much about keeping a house, having an adult relationship, or having a baby. I was very caught up in appearances—making things look normal, doing what was expected of us, and so forth. I did not have a very good relationship with his parents. The event I write about in this letter was when things really began to deteriorate. I've known for a long time that I created a tense relationship for several years. But since we reconciled with them before we divorced, and now they seem to have a good relationship with him and with my son, I hadn't sent this letter or previous versions until recently.

Dear Margie and Bill,

I have owed you this apology and explanation for a long time. When I was married to your son, I wanted you to think well of me. While we were first dating, he would tell me things you approved of and things you didn't. Church was good. Calling him by his nickname was bad. Race wasn't an issue for you. Sexual orientation was. I tried very hard to be a good Catholic girl. I didn't feel very good. I wasn't Catholic. And I was no longer a girl.

None of that really has anything to do with you, other than to set the context for my hurtful behavior. For some reason, I felt like you judged me and found me lacking. I wasn't a suitable future spouse for your son. Perhaps I just made all this up in my head. But in any case, it's how I felt at the time.

Then your son and I did the unthinkable. We moved our October wedding up to April and invited you to it one week in advance. We needed to be able to qualify for financial aid so he could attend anesthesia school. We were already engaged and pretty much living together, so it didn't seem like a big deal to us. I wouldn't get my ideal wedding, but he'd get his dream of becoming an anesthetist, and I'd look good as the supportive fiancé/girlfriend (see how it was all about appearances?). I'm not sure what you thought was going on. Maybe you wondered if I was pregnant. Whatever your thoughts and feelings, it was clear by your remarks at our wedding that you were highly displeased with us. I felt like you never really forgave me for that, like somehow you thought that it was entirely my fault. Your son was forgiven because he was your son, but I was forever guilty in your sight. This is how I felt.

So when Skip was diagnosed with Hodgkin's lymphoma less than a year into our marriage, and you asked if I needed help or wanted you to be there, I answered honestly, "No thank you, I'll be fine." I hadn't asked my own parents to come, though I spoke with them on the phone quite a bit. I certainly didn't want to feel your disapproval during a stressful time. I felt like I was doing all I could do to hold myself together. I was a full-time student and employee. We had a small one-bedroom apartment and a wild little dog. I was embarrassed by our life. I didn't feel like a good wife.

A day or so after Skip's second surgery, I called from work to let him know I'd be over at the hospital soon. He told me you were there. I went into panic mode. All I could think about was the unmade bed, the dog hair on the sofa and floor, no food in the fridge, a mess in the bathroom, and dirty clothes on the closet floor. I felt shy to see you, knowing I'd said

I didn't want you to come, but now you were here. I didn't go to the hospital. I went home. I took the dog out, came back inside, flopped onto our futon bed, and wept into my pillow. I cried myself to sleep, exhausted from holding it together for the past several weeks. I woke to the phone ringing. It was you. I was shocked. The answering machine came on, or something happened that disconnected us, but not before I heard the tell-tale buzz that alerted me that you were downstairs at the security doors, calling to be let into the building. Now I was extremely panicked. I called Skip, hysterical, asking what to do. He said you'd go away after knocking for awhile. And you did. But you knew I was home because I'd answered the phone. I was trapped in deceit. I was humiliated, exhausted, angry, and terrified.

Thinking about it now, almost twenty years later, it seems so stupid. But I remember the terror and the guilt. I didn't know how to explain my behavior. I couldn't face you. I couldn't face myself, my cowardice, my poor housekeeping abilities, and my shallowness. So I projected all my self-judgment and loathing on you. I made you the "wrong" ones. How dare you come to my home uninvited?

Because I refused to see you, because I was so horrified by that experience, it tainted the way your son saw you. It became easy for him to side with me since I was the one he lived with. And I was the one changing his bandages, holding the urinal, and helping him in various other ways.

I know we reconciled with you before we divorced because I remember you visiting us after Jonathon was born. I also remember attending Skip's sister's wedding when Jonathon was young. And even though things seemed fine between us, I don't think I ever shared my frenzied state of mind (during Skip's illness) with you.

You were right to do what you needed to do as parents. Had I been more mature, I would have acknowledged my embarrassment at being caught in a messy home napping, and asked to meet you at a restaurant later. But the me back then didn't know about extreme honesty, strength in vulnerability, or authenticity over appearances.

Please forgive me for projecting my fears and judgment on you and for allowing you to miss out on years with your son. As the mother of a son, I understand now what that might have been like for you.

I wish you and your family the very best,
Sarah

✎ To Lake Tainter, My "Happy Place"

When Skip and I lived in our apartment in Minnesota, we became good friends with our next door neighbor, Kris. After we moved to Marquette, Michigan, she moved to Lake Tainter, in Wisconsin near Menomonie. I visited her several times. I am not sure why I have remembered this one event for so long and with such detail. Perhaps it's because I named it my "happy place" when I was in therapy. It had probably only been a year or so since this event when I began calling it that. In any case, it is a place I feel grateful to have visited, a memory I cherish.

Note: I sent this letter to Kris.

Dear Lake Tainter,

When I'm asked to think of my "happy place" or to think of a time when I felt at peace in the world, I think of that glorious moment with you. I was visiting my good friend Kris. She had a little home near your waters. I was traveling by myself, or perhaps with my little Boston terrier, Suki. It was morning, and Kris was still sleeping. I woke, had coffee, and saw an exercise routine written on her white board. It included running up and down the dock stairs ten times. I thought, "Why not?" It was a cool morning. So I began trotting up and down the stairs. I ended my last set at the top of the stairs and turned back, panting, to look out at you, Lake Tainter. You were mostly smooth, with just a few ripples on your surface. Your trees were all filled out—some might have begun to turn color. It was quiet. I could hear my heart beating. A line from a Sandi Patty song, "Oh Lord, my God, how majestic is your name in all the earth," kept going through my head. I felt complete: connected to Source, connected to myself, alive, ready, here and now.

When I think back on that moment, I feel the peaceful calm of you again. I feel my thoughts slow. I feel the beating of my heart. All is well. I am so grateful for that moment in my life. I love that it happened spontaneously. It is not related to a particular achievement. It is not related to a special purchase. I didn't have to pay thousands of dollars to go to some amazing retreat center, chant with a guru, or fast for a week. It reminds me to look for the sacred in the ordinary.

You, Lake Tainter, make me wonder how many people you have offered your gift of serenity to—how many people have accepted this gift? And how many other times has Nature offered me a gift—a beautiful sunset, the sound of a loon, the taste of the first wild strawberry—a gift that I didn't take time to receive? How often have I ignored, taken for granted, or even purposely shut out the blessings of nature?

I didn't know back then, on that morning, what an impact, what a memory being present to that moment—to you—was creating. But oh, how very thankful I have been so many times since then that I took the time to take in that splendid scene, listen to the music of my soul, and tune into my own heart beating.

Thank you, life!

Thank you, Lake Tainter!

The lessons I have learned from you are these:

Pause.
Smell the flowers.
Pet the animals.
Feed the birds.
Listen to the water flowing, gurgling, and gushing.
Learn the words to your favorite songs, verses, and poems.

Who knows what the future will bring? Who knows which simple pleasures might make a world of difference—to be able to recall them, relive them in our memories, and conjure them up in our minds?

I remember hearing about an Iranian hostage who recalled Bible verses and Sunday school songs from her youth when she was taken captive. These words and verses brought great comfort to her during that situation. My mother's favorite Bible verse is Philippians 4:8: "Finally, brethren, whatever is true, whatever is honorable, whatever is just, whatever is pure, whatever is lovely, whatever is gracious, if there is any excellence, if there is anything worthy of praise, think about these things."

And I humbly add: Notice these things.

With awareness and appreciation,
Sarah

To Angie and Brian, My Former Foster Children

Skip and I moved to Marquette, Michigan, after I graduated from the College of St. Catherine and he graduated from anesthesia school. When I was twenty-three years old, we became foster parents. I didn't have children of my own then. I didn't know much about raising kids. I attended the trainings, talked with the social worker, had our home inspected, and all the while held onto the belief that love would solve any problem (and quickly). Even though the experts and experienced foster parents talked about syndromes and issues, I naively believed we wouldn't have those problems. We were special. We had enough love to heal any child and any situation. I didn't realize how arrogant and ridiculous this was. And so, when things didn't go as I'd expected, I didn't know how to cope. I didn't want to think there was something wrong with me. I didn't want to feel wrong for my willingness to help. And so, I made the kids (Angie, age five, and Brian, age eight) wrong. And unfortunately, I let them know this, too.

Dear Angie and Brian,

You are adults now. The older of you is close to the age I was when I was briefly your foster mother. I hope you are both well—physically, emotionally, and spiritually. I feel very bad about some of the time we spent together and mostly about how that time ended.

I became a foster parent for partly loving and mostly selfish reasons. Both your foster father and I were adopted. He was in remission from cancer, and we weren't sure if we could have biological children. We decided to become foster parents with partial interest in adoption. I also became a foster mother because it seemed like the loving thing to do. We had a big home. My husband made plenty of money. We didn't have children of our own yet. And we had a supportive church community. It seemed like the perfect fit.

When we first met you, we fell madly in love. At that time, you had been abandoned by your parents, and it was looking like you might be available for adoption. Both of you were beautiful and bright. You quickly attached to us. We enjoyed playing games, reading stories, and choosing clothes for you to wear. The first few weeks were absolutely ideal. You were well-mannered. You even traveled with us over the holidays. You seemed to get along well with each other.

Then, I'm not sure what happened. I think, partially, I got worn out from "entertaining" you all the time. It's what I thought good moms did, but I wasn't used to having extra people in the house. I think you also felt more comfortable with us and so perhaps relaxed your manners a bit. In any case, we started experiencing some challenges: bed-wetting, lying, not eating, and defiance. My little dream world started to shatter, and I felt threatened. Maybe they wouldn't think we were good foster parents if you started getting in trouble at school. We told your case worker that we were starting to see some problems, and she arranged to have you assessed by a counselor.

In the meantime, I became increasingly frustrated with dawdling, picky eating, and disobedience. We also learned that your father was back in town and was interested in having you sent to live with his parents. I think I started to give up on the situation at this point. I stopped believing that I could make a difference in your life. I allowed myself to become distracted by your presenting behaviors and forgot about your potential and who you really were on the inside. I became impatient.

One day, while I was blow-drying your hair, Angie, I wasn't paying close enough attention, and I touched the dryer to your forehead. When you said,

"Ouch," I blamed it on you, saying something like, "If you wouldn't be so wiggly, that wouldn't have happened." Another time, we were coming down the stairs, and I was in a hurry. We were holding hands, and I went down the stairs so quickly that I pulled you down the last two stairs so you stumbled at the bottom. Again, I told you to be more careful, not accepting any responsibility for rushing you. We began to have battles every night at dinner when you wouldn't eat your food. One night, you threw up, and I made you eat a piece of your pizza that had some vomit on it to show you that you couldn't get away with making yourself sick to get out of eating dinner. All these incidents were so wrong. And I felt awful. I told the case worker that I didn't feel like I was a very good foster mother, that I worried that I'd say something mean or hurt you. I was told, "Some foster parents spank." I was also told, "These kids are in a much better place than they would be otherwise."

In the end, we said we were no longer willing to have you. And the worst part is that we told you that it was because of your behavior that we were choosing not to keep you any longer and that we thought that's why you'd been to so many different foster homes already.

Since you left our care, I have thought about you often. Every Christmas, I pull out the ornaments you made at school with your photos in them. I've stopped hanging them on a tree, but I see them when I go through the Christmas box, and I say a prayer for your well-being.

My husband has children your ages, same genders. And so I can imagine what you might look like and how old you are now.

I wonder if you remember our home and us. And if so, what you remember about it. I hope you remember the good times. I hope you remember when we told you how special you were and that you could do or be anything you wanted. I hope you have realized through the years, maybe in counseling, that we were not ready to be parents or foster parents and that it was our incompetence and lack of preparation, not your unlovability, that created the struggles in our household.

I'm so sorry for how I treated you and what I said to you. I know how hurtful words can replay in our minds over and over, reminding us of past failures or disappointments. I shudder to think of my nastiness affecting you for years after you left us.

We did inquire about you, within a year of your leaving. And we asked if there would be an opportunity to have contact with you, but the counselor thought it wouldn't be a good idea, and we were not given any information about you. I'm sorry this apology is coming so late. I'm sorry for any residual negativity my actions have caused you.

Again, I wish you all the best in your lives.

With apologies and regrets,
Sarah

To Me, the One Who Gave Birth

I conceived Jonathon while I was a foster parent. When the children left our care, before I knew I was pregnant, I decided I was unfit to be a mother. When I first saw the ultrasound of his heart beating, though, I began to claim my role as mother. It seemed like he chose me. And I was determined to rise to the occasion and be the best mom I could be for him.

Although I had experienced a rough pregnancy with morning sickness, dehydration, and hospitalization, I was determined to have a natural birth. I read books. I took classes. I made a birthing plan. I packed my bag. I readied the nursery. I knew what I wanted and how it was going to go.

I lived across the street from the hospital at that time. So I imagined that I'd wait at home, breathing correctly, until I was dilated to about an 8 and almost fully effaced and then walk across the street to deliver.

I went into labor Wednesday, December 6, while my husband was on call (as a nurse anesthetist). It was painless, but the contractions were coming pretty quickly. I called him to let him know. The next day, I moved some furniture and ran errands (instead of resting as the books recommend). I was excited and confident. Thursday evening, we were at home watching TV when a friend stopped by to see us. I told her how well things were going and "my plan." She smiled and said, "Well, it'll probably get more intense as the night goes on." She had been a childbirth educator. But I didn't believe her. It might be that way for others, but it wasn't going to be like that for me. I had a plan.

By 9:30 or so that evening, things were still not very painful, and we decided to go to bed. By 11:00, I was in quite a bit of pain and no longer doing my easy, relaxed breathing. We timed the contractions and the amount of time in between and decided it was time to go over to the hospital. By the time we got out the door, I was cringing in pain and whimpering (to my dismay), so we nixed the walking over idea, and my husband went to get the car.

We arrived at the ER, and they wheeled me to a birthing room. I was checked and, to my horror, pronounced dilated to a 4 or some low number and barely effaced. Hearing that totally deflated my confidence. I was ready to have this baby. I was ready to push and be done with this intense pain. I was twenty-four years old.

Dear twenty-four-year-old, pregnant, giving birth Sarah,

Oh how I love you. I feel myself breathing deeply and pulling strength from the core of my being as I write to you. I remember the discouragement at hearing you were not ready to deliver yet. I remember the shower being too hot and then too cold. I remember the back pain, the cramping, and the intensity. I remember the music (music you'd planned specifically for relaxation and then pushing) was too loud and distracting. I remember crying out loud (and feeling embarrassed, but not being able to help myself). I remember looking over at the window in the room and thinking, "If I could just get myself over there, I could throw myself out. . . . It could be an option." And mostly I remember feeling abandoned—like there was no one with me who understood.

Twenty-four-year-old Sarah, I want you to know that I, thirty-eight-year-old Sarah, was with you then. I am with you. I know what a challenge that experience was. Somehow, the me I am today knew about that (because it's in my past) and was there with you during that time. You didn't feel me because you didn't yet know about me and listening to your various inner voices, but I was there. And I loved you through it all.

I know that one of the most frustrating parts for you was that the doctor who was on call for OB was not your favorite doctor. You didn't have much faith in her abilities because you'd heard stories from your husband about lawsuits. You heard her make comments about your not breathing correctly and wondering if you went to childbirth classes. That made you mad. The rebel in you, in both of us, just shut down. Later, you heard her complaining to a nurse about spilling coffee in the next room, and you thought (with great judgment and disdain), "You idiot! You're supposed to be in here helping me, and you're talking about spilled coffee!"

But you didn't say that. You didn't ask for what you needed. You didn't go to your "happy place." You closed your eyes tight, and you tried to pretend this wasn't happening. You hung on, in fear, between contractions and just wished away the painful experience that jerked you back into your body every minute or so.

I know how much you wanted things to be happening differently from the way they were. I know how much you wanted your husband to advocate for you. I know how much you felt betrayed by your own body. This was not the birthing experience you had planned. In a way, it felt like you were being raped by your own body, your own child. It felt violent and invasive and not at all what you wanted. And the people all around you were witnessing this as though it were no big deal.

After several hours of agony, your husband asked you if you wanted drugs, and you said yes. And you felt awful about it—like you had failed. And you wondered if they'd have a negative effect on the baby, but at that point you thought if you didn't have something, there wouldn't be a baby because you'd be dead.

The rest of the birthing experience is blurrier for you because you were drugged and exhausted. You weren't in so much pain, but you just wanted it to be over so you could go to sleep. You followed directions, breathing when they told you to and how they told you to. Then it was time to push. You thought you'd push a few times, and out he'd pop. Wrong! Because of the drugs and your weariness, it took a long time. After you'd been pushing for two hours, a new doctor came onto the morning shift at 7:00. You were thrilled, as this was your favorite OB physician from your prenatal visits. You had confidence in his abilities and appreciated his bedside demeanor as well. At 7:45, your beautiful, soulful son was born.

Most of your attention shifted to him. You wanted to make sure he was okay. You wanted to do everything right, nurse him right away, hold him so he bonded with you. But you were nauseous from the anesthesia. You didn't take time to process how awful the experience was for you. I think you worried that it made you a bad person that you didn't have a lovely, natural story to tell. You never really mourned the loss of your ideal birthing experience. I wonder if you thought it was due punishment for how the foster care situation turned out. In any case, you suffered and didn't allow yourself the satisfaction of acknowledging this.

I want you to understand that you did everything just fine. You were scared. Your plans went awry. You didn't yet have the skills to cope well with change, disruption, or the sense of powerlessness. But I do, and I was with you, hurting for you, but also knowing that this experience would make you more compassionate and appreciative.

I love you, you idealistic, dreamy girl! You have such beautiful ideas and visions. I'm learning how to keep those alive and fan the flames so they manifest. I am still someone who likes things how I like them. I still have a tendency to be too polite, not asking for what I need, allowing others to make the important decisions, but now I will put my foot down when a line has been repetitively crossed. And I have learned how to advocate on behalf of my son.

You were not alone in that hospital room. You are *never* alone! All the parts of you are right beside you, loving you, cheering for you. Everything is going to be just fine! You rest now, dear one. You've had a big night and day. You have a lovely gift of a child in your arms. You also have the lovely gift of you within you. And I promise you, you'll learn how to take better and better care of both of these gifts.

With deep love,
Sarah

To the Ya Yas

I met the Ya Yas when I was pregnant with my son. One of them was a member of the church I was attending. We'd been friends for about a year or so. She attended a group that met regularly to share their stories, listen to inspirational readings, and support one another on their paths of personal growth. Over the years, this group shifted to include seven of us, all women. This group of women have seen me through my early parenting issues, divorce, single parenting, living off of the electrical grid with solar power, training for a marathon, remarriage, moving, homeschooling, job searching, living with a low income, and all manner of other joys and sorrows.

When Jonathon was about eight or nine, I was preparing to travel to Korea. These are the women I wanted to continue to be a part of my son's life even if I didn't return (I was afraid of flying over the ocean). I knew that these women knew me in a way that my husband (of not quite a year at that time) did not. I wanted my son to know who I was and to hear it from people who saw me and loved me.

The Ya Yas include Betsy, Colleen, Garee, Helen, Martha, and Mary. I meet with these women every week for our wisdom circle. We pass a "talking stick," share from our hearts, listen from our hearts, and honor the sacredness in each person's journey. I know who I am when I am with these women. I remember what I am here to do. I am inspired by their lives, their choices, their words.

There is probably some messiness in our group. I know we've had some hurts and misunderstandings. But I also believe that in our hearts, each of us has a deep awareness that we belong here, are accepted here, and can count on these women no matter what. I have two favorite friendship quotes. One is from the Femail Creations catalog: "A friend hears the song in my heart and sings it back to me when my memory fails." These women have done that for me time and time again. They have reminded me of my courage, my heart, my wisdom, and my strength. The other is from Dinah Maria Mulock Craik: "Oh, the comfort—the inexpressible comfort of feeling safe with a person—having neither to weigh thoughts nor measure words, but pouring them all right out, just as they are, chaff and grain together; certain that a faithful hand will take and sift them, keep what is worth keeping, and then with the breath of kindness blow the rest away." The Ya Yas do this for me as well!

I hope all women have women friends like these. I know I am a better person and the world is a better place because of my Ya Yas.

Dear Ya Yas,

You know my heart. Sometimes, I think you may know it better than I do. You have listened to me share my stories since my almost fourteen-year-old son was in my womb. You have witnessed my struggles. You have witnessed my triumphs. You've seen me cry and laugh, yell and swear, hoot and holler, giggle and tell dirty jokes, share secrets and uncover dreams. You are my sisters, my dear friends.

I am so grateful for our connection. It truly amazes me. How can we come from such different places and yet be so similar? How can our journeys be so intertwined, and yet we are each so wonderfully unique? It's amazing, delightful, comforting, and one of the best gifts in my life to experience our friendship, our sacred connection. I believe our souls must have made some sort of contract with one another before we came into these lives. "Let's all meet and gather, beginning in the mid-1990s. That way, we'll be able to support one another through everything." And we did. And we have.

If my son and my husbands, my other friends, my business colleagues, my parents and siblings—if all the other important people in my life only knew how many times this group helped me figure out something in one of those relationships, they'd be astonished and grateful. I know I am a different person because of our group. You model for me a healthy and loving way of being. You are wives and mothers, bosses and employees, friends of others, sisters and daughters, artists and advocates. You are entrepreneurs and athletes. You are everything I want to be when I grow up. And because of my connection to you, I'm growing up to be exactly who I want to be!

What do I love most about us? I love that there is such freedom in our circle. I love that we have a structure for meeting regularly, and some of us have almost always done that. Others of us have drifted away for various reasons, not able or wanting to connect weekly. And yet the circle continues. And for those who go, it is a source of whatever is needed. It is a place to connect to Source, Self, and Sisters. We are always welcome and always appreciated. We meet in other ways as well: birthdays, movies, dances, concerts, hikes, church services, writing dates, road trips, law of attraction groups, and so forth. Not all of us are a part of every event or other group, and that is not a problem.

I love that we talk about the things that really matter to us. We share from our hearts and listen from our hearts. We set aside any judgments that might arise and enter with the highest intentions for one another. I love us! I love the me I am when I am with you!

Thank you, Ya Yas, for being exactly who you are and for loving me exactly as I am. You are a treasured gift in my life. I trust I am that for you as well.

Much love,
Ya Ya Sarah

⌂ To Chris and Jen on Moon Mountain

When my son was four, I'd been separated from my first husband for two years. I decided to rent a place off the (electrical) grid. It required us to heat our home with wood, use propane lamps and appliances, and snowshoe in about a mile or so during the winter. As challenging as some of those physical issues were, it is the people who stand out in my memory of that time.

I rented a tiny circular home with a loft. A family with two young boys lived on the property in an even tinier home. During my stay there, we became close friends, caring for one another's children, doing yoga, having saunas together, sharing meals, and getting to know one another. Before moving there, I had a certain image of who these people were. I thought they were very natural people who lived extremely basic lives—clean and pure and good. I thought they were better than me because I imagined that they only ate organic foods, wore natural fibers, and recycled everything. I was drawn to what I imagined was both simplicity and hardship, sort of like *Little House on the Prairie*. I put Chris and Jen up on the Pedestal of Perfection. When I began to see them as real people, with faults and insecurities, I felt disappointed. I never shared this with them. Instead, I gradually left the mountain and stopped visiting.

Dear Chris and Jen,

I lived near you for just nine months, but my time on the mountain has had a big impact on me. And of course, it's where I met my current husband, Chris. My primary motivation for moving there was my oncoming divorce. I thought I would need to figure out a way to live with much less income. And the hardships I imagined appealed to the puritanical side of me that thought I ought to be punished for the sin of divorce and that I needed to prove myself as the best parent to raise my son. And so I entered your world with something to prove: an inner and outer quest.

You were so welcoming at first. You were so supportive. If I hadn't felt that initial welcoming, I would never have stayed. I wanted you to like me. I wanted you to find me worthy of living with you. I wanted to impress others as well and show them what a hardy person I was.

Living there was both the most natural, easiest way of living and the most challenging, difficult time I've ever had. Life was simple: keep warm, make food, and take care of my son and dog. Life was difficult: split wood, keep the fires going, bring groceries in on a sled, carry out dirty laundry and trash on a sled, and plan for an hour-long or more hike from the car to the homestead.

Being the only single person and the newest to the community, I decided that I should just go along with whatever was customary. So when you all told me what to buy and cook and how to discipline my son and what to wear, I listened. And in many ways, I learned a great deal. A lot of your advice helped me stay warmer than I might have been. But I gave my power and my discernment over to you. I didn't listen to my own heart. I decided you must know best, as you've been living like this longer than I had. I sought your approval over my own.

Towards the end of my stay, I began to see some discrepancies in the advice you gave me and the way you lived. I found candy bar wrappers in your car. I saw you go through the drive-through at McDonald's. I heard you yelling at your children. All of these are typical American behaviors. It just wasn't how I thought of you. And I decided that I had been "tricked" into thinking you were different than you were. Notice, I did *not* take personal responsibility for myself, just blamed you instead. Now I recognize that we all have areas where we have ideals that we don't honor 100 percent of the time. It is part of our dance between divine and human.

I want you to know that I appreciate your support during my stay on the mountain. I would not have made it without you! I'm sorry that I wasn't mature enough to see that it was *me* who had given away my power, not you who sought to take it. I willingly gave you permission and encouraged you to be in charge of my life and guide me. When it didn't fit, I didn't have the courage to tell you. I thought disagreeing on principles and beliefs meant one of us had to be wrong, and I didn't want it to be either of us, so I just blamed you internally and left the relationship out the back door.

I want you to know that I felt really connected to you, and I care about you. I am genuinely interested in how you are. I would like to have a closer relationship again, heal any remaining messiness between us, and celebrate our time together.

With love and fond memories,
Sarah

To Ann, a Woman in an Emotionally Abusive Relationship

I find myself breathing faster as I write this introduction. I also notice that I'm swallowing more often. Although I don't regret my first marriage, I do regret my behavior in this relationship. I also have compassion for myself and understanding about my own fears. I still feel scared to have this one published. I fear that the man I mention might hunt me down and confront me or that women friends might think less of me, knowing I did not do all I knew to do for a friend and wondering if I would have risked more for them.

My extreme truth is that I don't honestly know if I would do anything differently. I sure hope I would. I think I have resources today that I didn't have then. I also have a greater sense of security living with my husband and "guard dog." But do we honestly ever know how we'll behave in a risky, traumatic situation?

After my experience on Moon Mountain, I returned to my home in town briefly before it sold. Then I moved to a nearby town and lived in an apartment owned by a homeschooling family we'd befriended. Jonathon and I lived there for almost two years.

Dear Ann,

This letter is way over due! I have thought about you and about writing something like this for years. It has been almost six years since I fled my rental at your place and abandoned our friendship as well. First of all, I hope you are okay. I hope you are healthy and happy and fulfilled. I hope your children are well and that you love who they have become. And most of all, I hope you feel safe and cherished in your home and in your marriage.

As your friend and tenant, I witnessed parts of your family life that troubled me greatly, but I never had the courage to talk with you about it or ask you if you were okay. I also witnessed a lot of family togetherness and a few tender moments. So I justified my silence as staying out of what wasn't any of my business. I told myself that I was just too sensitive and that it was my judgment of your husband's behavior that was wrong, not his behavior. And I told myself that both his mother and your mother witnessed his behavior and they didn't seem concerned, so maybe nothing was really wrong. But my intuition was screaming that your situation was not healthy or safe.

Now, six years later, here is my truth about your situation, the way I saw it. From my perspective, you tolerated and accepted an emotionally abusive man. I heard him screaming at his employees, you, and sometimes the kids. It never looked like there was any physical violence, so it was much easier for me to stay quiet, but I still feel that it was wrong. If I was scared to ask you about the situation, I can only imagine how frightened you must have been to be living in that situation. And perhaps my silence, living right next door, made it seem like how he was behaving must be normal.

I'm sorry, Ann. I'm sorry that I didn't have the courage to let you know I was concerned about you. I was afraid it would embarrass you. I was afraid you would deny it and be mad at me. I was afraid you might tell him, and he might become verbally abusive towards me. That is what finally made me leave: hearing him scream about me with only a thin wall between us. It frightened me to imagine him that upset with me, living so close. So I never slept there by myself again.

I left what was an unhealthy living situation for me when I wasn't even able to talk about it with you. It opened my eyes to the lack of integrity I had around my beliefs about community, my belief that "we are all one." I did not walk my talk. When it came right down to it, I protected myself and my child and left you and your children behind.

I live with these thoughts. And while I believe your family has moved away now, and that makes it somewhat easier for me to not feel guilty, I still care about you and your children. In the past, I have made myself feel better by criticizing your husband and congratulating myself for getting the hell out of there. But that's only to cover what I know in my heart troubles me: that I left you there, knowing what I knew (or thought I knew), never saying anything. I colluded with the secret of abuse. And I am ashamed of this.

I hope that anyone reading this now who is in a similar situation, either like mine or like yours, will find the courage to get support. It can be easy to say, "But he never hits me." But I am saying, publicly, that no human being should ever be screamed at, raged at, or frightened by someone else's emotional outburst. That is not healthy communication. That is out of control and inappropriate behavior. Sure, we all need to vent, but not directly at children or with children as witnesses. And when one person has the money and the power in a relationship, it makes it very difficult for the other person to feel they have a right to complain. No one deserves to be treated disrespectfully! It is wrong. We all know this on some level. And yet we pretend sometimes, when we have done it, or when someone we have chosen to be with does it to us—and it's too scary to tell ourselves the truth—that it's not that big of a deal. Our emotional safety is a huge deal!

Ann, again, I apologize for my lack of courage.

With humility and shame,
Sarah

✉ To Christopher on the Day of Our Wedding

I met Christopher when I lived on Moon Mountain. I had been separated from Skip for almost three years. Our relationship began with letters. Even when we were able to talk on the phone, we continued to write to one another for some time.

We dated for about two years before we were engaged on February 14, 2003. When I left my apartment near Ann, I moved in with Chris in the summer of 2003. We were married in my parents' backyard on August 1, 2004. This is a letter similar to the one I wrote to him on the day of our wedding. We can't find the original.

I include this not because it demonstrates any kind of cleaning up between us, but so you, Reader, can get an idea of who he is. Our relationship has grown to a place of honesty and vulnerability. We regularly have what we call "courageous conversations" about potentially risky topics such as death and dying, finances, and sex.

With both my husband and my son, I try my best to say what needs to be said each day in order to come clean. This includes apologizing, asking for clarification, sharing my feelings, and hearing what they have to say (even when they are not saying much). This is one of the best legacies I can imagine: clean, clear communication on a daily basis.

Dearest Christopher,

Today, we will pledge our love to one another, with our parents, siblings, and children as our witnesses. We have already pledged our love to one another in private. Our hearts and our lives have already begun the process of intermingling.

You have brought me so many gifts and lessons. I am so grateful for our time together so far. I am looking forward to many more years together! You are my partner and friend, my lover and soulmate. I am blessed by having been loved by you. Your calmness and groundedness made it safe for me to return to my natural self.

I have written many letters and journals to you. As you reread these, please hear the love in my words. And then, as that poem says, with the breath of kindness, blow the rest away. We are starting a new chapter in our story, one I want to end with "happily ever after."

I want to be someone who encourages you, challenges you to be the best person you can be, supports your wildest dreams and highest hopes, sees you, hears you, and through it all loves you. I want you to be this for me as well. I think we're off to a great start!

Your vision of the Triad of Triads is so beautiful. I want that for us, too! Thank you for partnering with me, homesteading with me, supporting me in raising my son, and loving me.

Your bride,
Sarah

To Nancy, My Husband's Ex-Wife

This is one of the letters I started towards the beginning of my letter-writing journey. As you might imagine, I started and stopped, wrote and rewrote, searching for words that were honest and compassionate, real and intentional. I hoped to send this letter around Thanksgiving. However, I decided to wait until the letters to Chris's children were complete. During that time, Nancy sent an e-mail to Chris that made me realize I needed to send this immediately. I could no longer afford to wait to have polished, "perfect" letters to express my feelings about an imperfect situation. I needed to trust my heart. I needed to trust Nancy's willingness to hear me.

I included two letters. The first letter was to explain why I was choosing to send the letter written during this process.

Dear Nancy,

I have been working on a letter to you for most of this year. It is part of a spiritual letter-writing process I have created to help me heal from my past and "come clean" with myself. I intended to send it to you for Thanksgiving, along with letters to Jesse and Anna. However, the letters to them didn't feel complete yet (too much of my own baggage included), and so I have waited to send your letter while I rewrite again and again various versions to Anna and Jesse.

This morning, I became aware that the situation in our blended family is as difficult and hurtful as it has ever been. I regret not having sent these sooner. I know that I run the risk of looking reactionary or defensive now. But truthfully, these letters have been in process since about April of this year.

I felt such hope when I saw you at church the other day and we said hello to one another. I came home and told Chris, "I wonder if I should just send Nancy's letter first." Again, I have waited because I have had such hope (and ego) that if I write the perfect letter, all will be well. People will understand and forgive one another. We can start by creating a new way of communicating with each other.

I don't feel like I can wait any longer. I want you to know what is in my heart. I hurt for our blended family, too. It hurts me, too, that Chris and Anna and all of us have such fragile relationships. I know that I bear some of the responsibility for that. And I am extremely sorry that I wasn't a better person when we all met. I believe we have all done the best we've known how, each of us striving to protect ourselves and be as understanding and compassionate as we've been able towards the other family members. Unfortunately, as unhealed people, we've had good intentions but have made lots of mistakes and experienced huge misunderstandings.

A part of me knows that a part of you will resist reading this letter with an open heart. I implore your spirit, Nancy, the part of you that believes in the good of all people. Please continue reading and know that I am on the side of light and love, healing, forgiveness, truth, and compassion. I am e-mailing Anna a letter as well.

May there be peace in Big Creek Valley and peace in each of our hearts.

Much love,
Sarah

Dear Nancy,

The light in me greets the light in you. So often, too often, we have connected and then disconnected false self to false self, ego to ego—fearful, cautious, concerned, and from a place of pain and distrust. I am sorry for my contribution to the stress and struggle of our blended families.

When I read what you've written in the newspaper or for local publications, I think, "Wow, we are so much alike." And I remember when I was just getting to know your children, we discovered so many similarities between your family and mine (especially my mom). And many of the books I was reading or loved were ones your children had seen on their bookshelves at home.

I also remember thinking—and perhaps I even e-mailed you this—that healing and transformation would begin with us. Something in me (could be my ego or female pride) believed that if you and I could get real with ourselves and each other, our families would fall in line. We would be the examples for our children. They would see as much love and possibility as we could "allow." Now, I realize that your children are adults, but I don't think it matters. I still catch myself taking my cues from my parents when I go to Wisconsin to visit. No matter how old we grow, we're still our mother and father's daughters. So I write this to you with great hope for forgiveness and healing.

Although we have never spent time alone together, I have many ideas about who I think you might be. Here are some of the stories I have created about you. I am choosing to share them with you in the hope that you might also see how similar we are. As a woman, married to the same man you were married to for almost twenty years, I can imagine that your female, artist soul might have felt unheard and unseen. As a mother, I imagine that your own hopes and dreams of serving the world in big ways may have felt limited and that you may have felt like your wings were clipped. From the little I know about your travels, I have made the assumption that you were and are more adventurous than I. And so I can only imagine that country life in the Upper Peninsula may have been even more limiting and frustrating for you than it has sometimes been for me. I also know that you came into motherhood at a later age than I. So I assume that you had a better sense of who you were and what your life was about and that the demands of motherhood and homesteading and marriage often pulled you away from your own self.

And though I know little about the dark time in your life, I know that it had something to do with feeling betrayed and abandoned by your closest friends. I know that it shook you to your core. I have heard you talk about what a difficult time this was for your family and how bad you have felt about the impact on your children.

And being divorced myself, I understand the deep sense of loss (even when what you had was not what you wanted) that comes with letting go of the hopes and dreams of a marriage, a primary relationship. I also understand the second-guessing about if this is what is best for the children. And I understand the fine line between owning my part and honoring my feelings.

I can see your innocence: the part of you that is doing the best you know how, that loves your children, that wants to move past all the hurt and pain of your relationship with your ex-husband. In the past, I have been full of blame and judgment. I have harbored resentment in my heart towards you. I have blamed you for situations with your children. I have blamed you for the way I felt about things. I have not always taken responsibility for my part in our blended family situation. I have acted like I was a victim of your home's "culture." I got caught up in the differences in our ideas about communication, schedules, requests, permission, and so forth. I see now how my own negative feelings about our situation contributed to a vicious cycle of distrust, miscommunication, lack of compassion, and finally abandonment of relationships.

I don't pretend to know how to make things better. I am not so naive to think that there's one solution that will make everyone happy. I used to believe we all needed to sit down together, maybe with a counselor, and hash everything out in the open—make sure everyone was heard, go through a whole forgiveness and healing ritual, and make agreements about what we wanted, what we were willing to do, and how we wanted to be together. Now I am able to breathe more spaciousness into what happens and how healing occurs. I do know that I want healing for myself and for all involved.

I know that I think of all of us as a large, blended family. And I want to feel free in our family, and I want others to feel free as well. I want our family to be a safe environment where people are free to share their feelings and know that they will be heard—not necessarily agreed with, but heard and respected. I want our family to be a place where we do more than make small talk with one another and act politely.

There's a saying: "How you do anything is how you do everything." I want us to "do" our family with love and grace and ease. I want us to see to the heart of each member and find that person innocent and worthy. I want us to relate to one another as part of a larger spiritual family, not just people who through marriage and divorce and remarriage happened to end up in a similar neck of the woods. We are in each other's lives for a reason. We are in each other's lives to heal ourselves and heal one another. I see this as an opportunity to live what I believe about living courageously, trusting the universe will provide support, letting my heart find a way when the way isn't obvious, and being willing to risk and risk again for the sake of love.

I read a story recently about two angels walking through the halls of heaven. They come to a scene where someone is being forgiven by someone else for a horrible act. God says that this is the greatest gift you can give, the gift of forgiveness. One of the angels says something like, "I want to be able to give that gift." And God replies that in order to give that gift, someone must love you enough to hurt you deeply enough that it will require your forgiveness. The angel wonders aloud who would love her that much. The other angel says, "I love you enough to do that for you." The first angel is deeply moved and thanks the second angel, saying, "And what can I do for you, in appreciation for this great gift you are willing to give me?" The second angel says, "When I hurt you, look into my eyes, and remember who I am." Perhaps we made a pact like this, Nancy. Perhaps we both knew, as angels, that in order to grow, heal, learn, and give what we wanted to in this life, we both needed and wanted to give the gift of forgiveness. And in order to give that gift, we each needed to be hurt. My angel self loved you enough to be willing to give and receive this gift. My human self is beginning to see and remember my angel self and your angel self as well.

Will you take my hand, offered in peace, and leap with me into this murky, messy space that is our family right now—and breathe with me and send healing, loving thoughts with me, and together, look for a way through to love and with love?

In peace,
Sarah

To Anna and Jesse, My Husband's Children

In the beginning of my relationship with Chris, all of our children seemed to accept our dating and relationship fairly well. We traveled, had overnights, and celebrated holidays together. Then, as the children got older and we got more serious about each other, the relationships and our blended family dynamic began to change. By the time we were married, there was clearly some stress in certain relationships and in the family as a whole. Now, five years later, there are large chasms between some of us and deep animosity between others. I feel sad, angry, disappointed, and embarrassed about much of our family situation. I also feel grateful, proud, and hopeful about other parts.

I live with my husband and my son. So we have ongoing discussions, challenges, celebrations, and conversations. I do not live with or communicate much (or at all) with my husband's children. If this book truly is to be my bucket list of cleaning up relationships, then I know I need to include this letter. And yet I have struggled with it. Many of the other difficult areas of my life are about situations that are done. I will be in relationship with these two people for at least the rest of their dad's life (assuming he dies first, as he's twenty-two years older than I). What I write here, in many ways, could have a much bigger impact on the present and future than my other letters that are exclusively about the past. I want it to be just as honest, just as clean and clear, vulnerable and real.

As I was in the process of drafting various versions of letters to Anna and Jesse, together and separately, I learned that the situation was even worse than I thought. I felt I needed to take immediate action. So I sent separate letters, written in one day instead of over a year. I'm including both the last version of the letter written to both of them and the separate letters I actually sent.

Dear Anna and Jesse,

It's been a long time since I've written anything to either of you. I find that I'm not sure where to begin. I guess I'll begin with my hopes. What do I hope for? I hope that one day, we'll be able to sit down and listen to each other's stories—really listen, heart to heart. And we will be able to step into each other's stories while they're being told and really see with each other's eyes and feel with each other's hearts. And because we are able to do this, we'll then be able to truly understand one another. From this place of understanding, we can create new stories, ones that include each of our previous stories and also point to the new story we want to create and tell about ourselves and one another. I hope that one day my heart will be pure enough that I can accept however you feel about me without being triggered to defensiveness or explaining. I have been actively moving in this direction for some time now. I hope that one day, all your dad's favorite people can sit in the same room, with loving hearts and generous natures, offering true forgiveness and acceptance. I hope that we all experience individual happiness and happiness as a family.

What do I regret? I regret that I was not surer of myself and stronger in my spirituality when we met. I wish that I was then the person I am now. With greater confidence, I would have worried less about what you thought of me and more about how we were all truly doing as a family. I would have been less concerned about giving the right gifts, planning vacations, preparing meals, and keeping the house clean and more concerned with the quality of the relationships that were being formed. I regret that I felt threatened by your rejecting me. When I discovered how deep your animosity was towards me, I reacted in fear, instead of responding with love. I allowed it to justify my pulling away from you. I allowed it to create doubt about whether or not your dad and I were right for each other. Those thoughts then stressed our marriage, which made our relationship and getting things solid with us the primary focus during a time when you really needed us (at least him) to be more present and available for you. I regret that I let myself go to the "victim" place of hurt and anger and feeling wronged, so that I came to avoid interactions with you. I no longer reached out to you or encouraged your dad to reach out. I constricted my heart and let you experience the "natural consequences" of not accepting me or respecting my requests. That was passive aggressive. That was me playing small and being vindictive. I feel embarrassed and ashamed that I behaved that way. I also have compassion towards the part of me that reacted in that way. I know my hurt and fear back then. And I hope someday you will be able to see the vulnerable side of me as well. It does *not* excuse me. As an adult, I believe I had a greater responsibility for creating harmonious relationships in our family than you.

The ironic thing is that I genuinely cared about you and really wanted you to love me. My neediness for your love and acceptance tarnished my pure intentions. I was manipulative. I tried my best to make you love me by buying you what I thought would be amazing gifts, taking you places I thought would be special, and making our home a place you felt welcome. But I didn't feel like anything I did was good enough. I felt judged and found lacking. I felt not smart enough, not fun enough, and not generous enough. And it made me work even harder at "earning" your love for awhile. Then when I discovered that you didn't like how I was with you and had complaints about me, I couldn't take it. My fragile ego self was so hurt that I couldn't hear the truth or the hurt or the hope in your complaints and criticisms.

I don't want to dwell on the past, except to say that I regret that I wasn't a better person, fuller of love and acceptance for myself, so that I wasn't so attached to receiving it from you. It is neither your responsibility nor your obligation to like me or accept me. If I loved myself enough, like I do now, then although I would still want you to like me and accept me, I wouldn't feel that I needed your acceptance and approval. I was not honest in the beginning of our relationship, not with your dad or with you. I wasn't focused on honesty. I was focused on approval. Basically, I was sick.

So where do we go from here? Well, as I said in the beginning, I'd love to really be able to hear how it's been for you. And then I'd love to start over, creating something from a place of free individuals deciding how they want to be together (or not) in a way that feels good to all.

Your dad has been offering his love to you all this time in the best ways he knows how. He is a simple man. Things just aren't that complicated for him. He loves the two of you. He would love to spend more time with you. But he won't ever force that. One of the primary indicators of true love is freedom. Your dad is a master at loving with freedom. When he loves someone, he really loves and accepts them just as they are. He doesn't have an "improvement plan" in mind. He hopes we will be the best people we can be. He tries to be that himself. But he will not intervene with our freedom to choose, kind of like God that way.

I'm rambling. The bottom line is that things feel awkward at least and hostile at worst between us. I want things to at least feel healed and at best feel happy and free. I care so much about both of you. I want you to have a strong family foundation. You don't have to like me. You don't have to accept me. I just ask that you not allow your feelings about me to interfere with your relationship with your dad.

With hope,
Sarah (your not-so-evil stepmother)

Dear Anna,

First and foremost, I am so sorry you are feeling so bad about your relationship with your dad and that you feel so unwelcome and horrible about coming to our house and seeing me. I guess I naively believed that we were beginning to heal when you hugged me at your graduation and asked me to take a photo of you and your dad.

I don't want you to feel wrong for any of your feelings. And I don't want you to feel you're to blame. We all created this situation. The adults, your parents and I, are mostly responsible, as we could have set the tone for healthy, open conversations that allowed you and Jesse to just be kids. We didn't.

This past year, I have written many letters to you and Jesse, trying to find the right words to express my apologies for my part in our blended family dysfunction and my hope for how I'd like things to be. I have really struggled with this, as my tendency has either been to take all the blame myself or to make myself look like my intentions were always only pure. Neither of these positions are true or real. I absolutely am responsible for the choices I made, the things I said, the way I felt, the way I communicated, and the beliefs I held. Unfortunately, I know that I was very focused on winning you and Jesse over in the beginning and getting you to like me. These are not pure intentions. I felt insecure about my relationship with Chris—that if he didn't think you liked and accepted me, he wouldn't like me anymore either. So even though a lot of what I did was because I loved you two and wanted to be generous and kind, other parts had a manipulative flavor— trying to earn your love and prove to myself and to you that I was a nice, good person.

When I discovered that you resented me, I reacted with hurt instead of responding with love. I felt like you rejected me and all my attempts to be your friend. I felt like I had done everything "right." I'd been generous and kind and accepting, and then because I'd stated some preferences and made some requests, I'd been totally rejected.

Anna, you were right to feel whatever you were feeling and let your parents know how you felt. I wasn't mature enough to see you as a young woman asserting herself. I took it personally, felt attacked, and began to withdraw my love and attention. I began to see you as a threat to my relationship with Chris. I tried to pretend that everything was fine, but I resented you for rejecting me.

I justified distancing myself from you as self-protection and letting you and your dad figure out your own relationship. I'd just stay out of it. Really, I was punishing you. I was withdrawing my love and attention in an attempt to make you see how nice I had been and what you were missing since you'd decided I was the wicked stepmother. This was vindictive and small. I thought (hoped) you'd see that you were wrong about me and apologize.

I wish I had been a bigger person to see to your heart and understand your pain. I got distracted by the "presenting behaviors" I judged as withdrawal, rejection, and manipulation. I see now that you wanted what every child wants: a family where they feel loved and seen and heard. For awhile, we didn't give you that. I didn't give you that. I was so focused on my own experience—my own fears of not being loved, seen, and heard—that I didn't see you as you. I was the adult. I should have been able to be big enough to get over any personal hurt and be there for you. I am seeing you now. I am hearing you now. And my response is compassion, deep compassion for the hurt parts of you and deep hope for the parts of you willing to heal and grow through this.

I want us to move past polite tolerance and get real with one another. I have shared a bit of what our troubled past has been like for me. I would love to hear what it has been like for you. I want to listen to you from my heart and give you the gift of finally being heard and seen, by me, without judgment. I want us to heal, individually and as a family. And I know I can only do my part. I have no control over anyone else.

I don't know how to say the next part without sounding like I'm scolding you. I am *not* trying to make you feel bad. But there is no one else to share with you what I want you to know: that your dad absolutely loves you! He spends a great deal of time thinking about you, sending you good thoughts, thinking of ways to reach out to you, and so forth. I know you haven't felt like he's been there for you. I want you to know that he has been here, reaching out. You want his love. He loves you. It's a match! I don't mean to discredit your feelings. You're entitled to believe what you want, feel how you want. *And* I could give you proof of my memories of tens to hundreds of times where a movie has reminded him of you or he's wondered if you'd like something, has looked over at your mom's house when passing by, etc. So you can feel rejected, and you can look for evidence to support that. Or you can feel his love and find evidence to support that. It's your choice.

I love you, Anna. I truly believe we are in this family, together, for some higher purpose. Before we came down to earth, we wanted to connect in this lifetime. We wanted to be a part of the same family. I know I can learn from you. I hope you can learn from me as well. Blended families and even nuclear families are work. Communication takes high intentions, practice, and a willingness to stay in the conversation, even when what we hear hurts our feelings or isn't what we wanted to hear. Please stay in the conversation! Let's call a "do over" and see one another with fresh eyes and listen to one another with fresh ears. Please see me for the person I am today, and not the person I was five years ago. I'm still far from perfect, but now I am willing to be honest, compassionate, and real.

Love,
Sarah

Dear Jesse,

Hi. How're you? It seems like we've been out of touch for quite awhile. That feels awkward to me, and I feel my old insecurities rising. I feel funny telling you this because I don't want you to feel like you're obligated to write to me or to feel guilty that you didn't respond. But I also want you to know that I think about you and Anna often. And I have been doing a lot of work on myself in an attempt to clean up messy relationships from my past and in my present. I feel very bad about the distance between us and between the two of you and your dad.

This past year, I have been on a spiritual journey—cleaning up my past through a letter-writing process. I have written many versions of letters to your mom, you, and Anna. I have been trying to see fully what happened between us, where I am responsible and need to make amends, and what I might be able to do to make things better in the future.

It's been challenging for me to balance what feels both honest and com-passionate (towards myself and towards you, your mom, and Anna). I want to honor all of our feelings and experiences, without making anyone wrong by pointing fingers. How do I find a way of seeing our large, blended family and each person in it that is honest, respectful, and loving?

I tend to bounce back and forth between feeling overly responsible: if I hadn't married Chris, if I'd had a healthier self-esteem, if I hadn't felt so threatened when Anna rejected me, if I had cared less about a clean house and more about you two feeling welcome here, and if I had been more spontaneous and not so attached to wanting to know when you'd be visit-ing—and then, on the other hand, I would blame you, your mom, and your sister. Neither of these extremes feels good. Self-blame makes me feel bad about myself. Blaming you makes me feel bad about myself. Both types of blaming keep me stuck in a small, scared place where I feel hurt and angry. This is *not* what I want for any of us.

I love you, Jesse. And I love your mom and sister, too. And the highest part of me can see that we are all doing the best we know how. It is no one's fault, *and* we created this situation together. I also believe we are capable of healing and growing together.

Will you forgive me for my smallness, my fears and insecurities, my judg-ment, and my intolerance? Will you share with me your hopes for how our family can heal and work with me to create a place where we all feel safe enough to be ourselves and loved enough to heal and free ourselves from the bonds of our old story?

I wish you were going to be home for the holidays. You will be missed even more this holiday season than we already miss you each day.

I also want you to know that if there is anything you want to or need to say to me, I would love to hear it. I know it might not be easy, but I believe open, honest, compassionate communication is the key to healing and growth in relationships.

Merry Christmas, Jesse!

Love,
Sarah

✍ To a Former Colleague
Who Owns a Pornography Business

I planned to include a letter that dealt with pornography and prostitution in this book. I've had experience as a partner, in two separate relationships, where the man used pornography or prostitutes or both. I have watched one pornographic movie. I have seen some pornographic magazines and photos. I have also coached a client who would talk or e-mail me about masturbating to pornography. My son was exposed to a classmate who would talk with him about pornography at school. I know I have had a wide range of emotions about all of this—from acceptance, shock, abhorrence, judgment, shame, etc. I know I need healing and closure around this topic. But whom do I write my letter to? Whom have I blamed? Where is there a constriction in my heart?

Just yesterday, I learned that a colleague of mine (we were in a six-month certification program together several years ago), whom I absolutely adored, runs a pornography business with her husband. This is a real live person I knew, at least a little. It feels easier to write to someone specific than to a broad category of people.

For the sake of anonymity, I'm going to call this woman Jane.

Dear Jane,

I can hardly begin to share with you the myriad thoughts racing through my head. I have just learned about the pornography business you and your husband operate. I am shocked. This news challenges all of my assumptions about you.

I have assumed that you made your money coaching. Now I assume your wealth comes from the pornography business. I have assumed that when you talked about wanting to help women in your country, that you meant a literacy program or using your coaching skills in some way. I now assume that was some sort of cover-up or justification for what you are really doing. I assume that some part of you knows that what you are doing is not right. I assume that another part of you thinks I'm an uptight Midwesterner who has no clue.

Let me tell you my experience. I've been hurt by a husband's use of pornography. I've felt angry at the women who post their photos. I've felt anger at people in the business. I've felt anger at my husband. I've felt anger at myself. I've blamed myself—if only I were prettier, thinner, and sexier. I've blamed my husband—if only he had more self-control, could be vulnerable, and got help. I've blamed the women who pose naked for photos—if only they had other choices, if only they wouldn't flaunt themselves. I've blamed the business—if only it was illegal. I've blamed the culture—if only we weren't so sexually repressed, things wouldn't have to come out in dark ways. All this blaming hasn't helped (no surprise there).

I don't blame you, either. I believe that if you thought you had another, better choice, you'd be making it. And I can even see how you could justify it (like I justified stealing): people are going to do it anyway; at least you really care about the women. If people didn't buy it, there wouldn't be a business. It was created by demand.

I'm listening to some Buddhist teaching CDs. They talk about what to do when you notice pain, discomfort, judgment, or any of the difficult emotions. They talk about breathing in the pain and then exhaling an intention. I am sitting here, breathing in my own pain—pain of betrayal, loss of innocence—exhaling a wish for peace in my heart. I am breathing in your pain—at having to constantly hide or justify your business in the coaching industry, where authenticity is the name of the game. It can't be easy or comfortable. I exhale a wish for peace in your heart. I now inhale the pain of all the women who are in this business by choice or by circumstance. And I exhale for them a wish for peace in their hearts. I inhale the pain of the men and women who buy services and products from this business. I breathe in their loneliness, fear, and pain. I exhale a wish for them for freedom in their hearts. Finally, I inhale again, the pain of all of us who are affected in any way by this topic—all our collective suffering. And I exhale a wish for peace in all our hearts, peace in all our relationships, peace in the entire world.

This is all I know how to do right now. I've learned (at least I hope I have) that I cannot control other people: my husband, you, anyone. And I can't make this situation better. There is pain here. But I can sit with it, acknowledge it, breathe it in, and finally exhale, with a wish for peace.

Blessings to you, Jane. I truly wish you and all of us peace in our hearts and peace in this world.

—Sarah

To Karen Kimsey-House, President and CEO of the Coaches Training Institute

In November 2005, I began my coach training with the Coaches Training Institute (CTI). I graduated from their Coaching Core Curriculum (2006), Certification Program (2007), and Leadership Program (2007). Throughout my time as one of their students, I experienced a broad range of feelings about their programs, their leaders, and myself. It reminds me of romantic love. I fell in love. I committed. The honeymoon ended, and I saw things differently. I began to look for the problems and what didn't work well. I returned to a state of love and appreciation by honoring the human and the divine in myself, the CTI leaders and staff, the CTI programs, and life itself. I came to realize that just because I experienced things a certain way did not mean CTI should change their programs. I know that what I learned about myself and others in their various programs and the connections I have made to lifetime friends have greatly affected me. It's time they knew this. Of the three cofounders, Karen is the only one I have had any kind of direct contact with. She is also the one I assume is most like me.

Dear Karen,

I haven't met you in person, but we spoke on the phone once, about the Prison Project. This letter has been roaming around in my head for a few years now. Like so many of my other letters, it's shifted as I've shifted and changed. In the beginning of my relationship with CTI, my letter would have been filled with awe and gratitude. It would contain multiple superlatives: a fabulous course, amazing leaders, incredible curriculum. Later, the letter might also contain some feedback about a moderately uncomfortable experience I had. Later yet, a letter might contain quite a bit of "here's where your courses don't work well for me." In fact, if you pull out my evaluation forms from the different courses I attended, I bet you'll be able to see this pattern.

It's been almost two years since I completed my final CTI program, leadership. Since graduation, I have thought off and on about what I liked and didn't like, what I'd do differently if I led a program for your organization, and what parts I'd use in creating my own curriculum. At this point, that doesn't seem relevant. It isn't what I most want to say to you.

Karen, I deeply appreciate you as a woman, as a creator, as a business person, and as a spiritual being. I recognize that you didn't found this company on your own. Nor did you create all the programs by yourself. However, I believe that you are the heart of CTI. And I believe that you were somehow responsible for the parts that made my experience positive.

In leadership, we're taught the skill of sharing our assumptions with someone for the sake of keeping the space between you and the other person clean and bright. I want to share my assumptions with you in hopes that you'll feel affirmed if you already see yourself this way and perhaps called forth if you don't yet see yourself this way.

I assume that a part of you knows the exact direction this company needs to go.

I assume that you are the heart of this organization. You bring compassion and groundedness.

I assume that you often play or allow yourself to be superficially satisfied with the role of "wind beneath the wings" *and* that you are genuinely a sweet, humble person.

I believe your voice does not always get heard, but it is precisely what is needed.

I believe that you're the one who "picks up the pieces" when things fall apart, even when the meltdown was not your responsibility.

I just want to say thank you. Thank you for pouring your heart into this work, trying (like water) to shape it, over time, into what's needed.

I do hope to meet you in person one day. I'd like to look into your eyes, see your soul, and thank that part of you for all the contributions you have made.

I do believe that CTI as a company is trying its very best to do what is right most of the time. I believe it'd be even more effective with stronger leadership from you.

In truth, love, and high intentions,
Sarah

To Camilla,
My Coach, My Spiritual Guide, My Friend

Camilla Rogers is a professional, certified coach. She is also a deeply spiritual woman with a heart of platinum! She is one of the purest, most real, and least ego-driven people I know. She has encouraged me, inspired me, supported me, helped me, grown me, challenged me, and through all this loved me deeply. I am forever grateful for her presence in my life. We have connected in a variety of ways. She supervised me during my coaching certification. She worked with me on the Laura Whitworth Prison Project. She has been my life coach for over a year. I hope that each of you has a Camilla in your life. I hope to be a Camilla in the lives of others.

Dearest Camilla,

I am so, so grateful for you! I know you know how much I love you. And I know we really don't have any "stuff" in our relationship. There's nothing that needs cleaning up between us. So why would I include a letter to you in this book? I feel that public affirmation of your gifts is needed.

You are like water for my soul. I am nourished by your love, your witnessing me, and your support. Because I know you and you know me, I have so much more hope for myself and for all humanity. I hear your stories, and I see who you are now. And I just want to celebrate your triumph of spirit, mind, and heart. You are a testament to faith and willingness. I deeply respect and admire you.

When we spent time together creating curriculum, I was drawn to you. But time and time again, my heroes have fallen off their pedestals. So I watched you closely. And I listened to your words. And I saw integrity, humility, willingness, and love. When I returned home, I kept thinking about you. I knew I wanted to pursue a coaching relationship with you. You have not disappointed me. You are genuine. The person you see is the person you experience. My experience with you continues to be enlightening, inspiring, sacred, honest, and true.

My wish is that everyone has a Camilla in their life. The world would be a much better place. Everyone would feel seen and be heard. People would have at least one relationship where they were safe to practice extreme honesty. People would know they had value. They would feel affirmed for who they are, not just what they do. They would be encouraged and supported to grow to their full potential and then some.

Oh, wonderful Camilla, do you think it's possible to clone you?

I'm so excited about your dream of bringing personal story gems to life, allowing people to create a multimedia presentation of a life story. I just know it will be a gift to all who choose to explore that path with you. I really enjoyed creating mine, using parts of the letter to my biological mom. Any and all time with you is a tremendous gift. I am so very, very grateful for your presence in my life.

Much love,
Sarah

To the Women of Denver Women's Correctional Facility

Most of the background for this letter is included in the letter. However, I do want to add that this experience was one of the motivations for writing these letters. I wanted to respond to the questions I was asked while I was at this facility. This led to my idea to embark on a spiritual journey of letter writing, to explore relationships with people and events and places that had a big impact on me. I will always be grateful to these women for their courage and curiosity. They inspired me to higher levels of extreme honesty.

Dear Women of Denver Women's Correctional Facility,

Hello. Please allow me to introduce (or reintroduce) myself. My name is Sarah. That's all I'm officially allowed to tell you (given the rule of offering only a first or last name). I have been at Denver Women's as a volunteer twice now. My first visit was in March 2008, when I assisted with a course offered by the Laura Whitworth Prison Project. I sat at the back of the room and witnessed the amazing strength, truth, and beauty in the women who participated in that course. I fell in love with you—with your courage to look at yourselves and your choices, with the compassion you have for one another, and with your willingness to allow us (outsiders) to share what we offer and to receive our words and our presence with such appreciation.

My second visit was December 2008. This time, I sat at the front of the room and co-led with my friend and colleague Helen. Again I witnessed amazing courage, vulnerability, and love. But I also noticed some resistance. And in both our evaluations and in one exercise you wondered what made us think we could teach you, why we wanted to do this work, what we had done that was bad, and how did we think we could relate to you.

Those words, those questions, are the reason I am writing to you—to all of you, but especially to those who attended any of the Laura Whitworth Prison Project courses (there was also one in August 2008 that I did not attend). I hope to answer your questions and answer some of my own. Why am I doing this work? What called me to serve women in prison? What makes me think I *am* serving you?

My dear sisters, woman to woman, we are united. When one of us is beaten, raped, jailed, belittled, or wronged in any way, so are we all. In that same way, when any one of us is exalted, celebrated, heard, honored, or cherished, so are we all. So, first and foremost, I come to you as a human being who happens to be a woman, an Asian woman. I was born in South Korea in 1971. I was given up for adoption when I was several weeks old. I had scabies (bugs in my scalp). I was malnourished (I had a somewhat distended belly for most of my childhood). I had a festering sore on the back of my head from being left to lie in dirty conditions. I had giardia (a parasitic worm usually found in feces). I needed a blood transfusion and head surgery. Thankfully, I was adopted by wonderful people who raised me in a clean, Christian, middle-class home in the Midwest. Even so, those early experiences are my roots, where I came from. And a part of me has always felt like I survived a situation that others did not survive. This survivor's guilt has triggered a longing in me to make something of myself.

For as long as I can remember, I've wondered what or who I would be when I grew up. I wondered this in my childhood. In my teens, I mostly wanted to be something that would look successful. In college, I changed majors seven or eight times and attended two different schools before I graduated. So it would be a complete lie for me to tell you that I have always wanted to work with women in prison, or with women, or in prison.

However, when I look back, I can definitely see some influences. I was raised in a home where we prayed for people in prison. I learned that Jesus befriended people from all walks of life. Later, in my early twenties, I volunteered at a jail as a GED preparation tutor. I continued tutoring there as part of an adult continuing education course.

But what was it that brought me to this work with you? Through a lengthy series of synchronistic events, I became a life coach. Most of my training was through the Coaches Training Institute, a company that a woman named Laura Whitworth cofounded with two other remarkable people. During my leadership training with the Institute, I was asked to develop a workshop. As I prepared, I thought about doing work with blended families, as that has been one of my biggest struggles. When it was my turn, I stepped to the front of the room to share my thoughts. I heard myself saying that I was going to create a program for people in prison. One of my leaders, a dear friend of Laura's, pulled me aside. Laura had died of cancer only the day before. Her friend told me that Laura's "bigger game" was around training prisoners to be coaches. I remembered then that my friend Helen had done that work with Laura. And that was the beginning of my connection with a project that had been on hold for a few years.

Another leadership student, Deanna, and I worked together to reenergize the Prison Project. She had always had a desire to serve marginalized populations. And so, together with others, we helped bring a group of people and these programs to you.

What qualifies me to be with you? My qualifications include a compassionate heart, a mind that understands concepts and can present them in basic language, and a belief in living a life of contribution. I want to make a difference and I will bloom where I'm planted (or transplanted).

I regret that it wasn't obvious that I felt called to be with you. I regret that I didn't seem more "leaderly" to you. I sometimes struggle with self-doubt. Am I the best person to be doing this work? I've decided that it doesn't matter. Until there are people beating down the doors to spend time with you in a compassionate way, I will do what needs to be done.

This work, human to human, sharing our journeys so that those following might have a road map to guide them, is my work. I want to leave the path cleaner, clearer, with well-marked signs and brochures explaining the trail system, warning of dangers, and highlighting the rare and beautiful.

You can journey through this time in a way that grows you towards who you want to be, who you truly are. Yours is the path of most women. Though we don't all end up in a physical prison, we're very good at making our own prisons out of the roles we play, like "good wife," "suburban mom," "beauty queen," "athlete," or "Christian." We box ourselves in so tight that many of us are suffocating. It's time for us to free ourselves from the bonds of our own making! Whether or not we can be physically free, our spirits can be free by choice.

This is what I want for you. Remember the poem I read you in December, about true freedom—from addiction, limiting beliefs, regret, self-induced pain, freedom to make conscious choices that serve your good and the good of all? There is good. There is truth. There is beauty in each one of us. Seek, and ye shall find. Knock, and the door will open. Believe you are here for a reason. Our life paths crossed for a reason. I had a gift for you. You had a gift for me. Much of life is this: the exchanging of gifts.

Next time I come, I hope to receive your gifts. And I hope you receive mine as well.

Until then, look within for a glimpse of your dancing star! I know it's there. Find it, hold it, and let it shine!

With love and hope,
Sarah

To the Buffalo, My Leadership Tribe

I am a member of the Buffalo Leadership Tribe. We attended four retreats over ten months together, from the fall of 2006 to the fall of 2007. The retreats included experiential exercises like trust falls and high ropes courses. They included learning a leadership model. They included giving presentations, creating and delivering workshops (alone and together), and being "typed." Through it all, I was most focused on being seen as a good and powerful leader. I wanted to be chosen to lead programs for the training organization, the Coaches Training Institute. I loved my tribe mates, and some became good friends. But what justified the cost to me was the potential for a leadership opportunity.

Now, three years later, I realize that the greatest learning and gifts were not the professional ones I hoped to receive. Instead, it is this community of shining spirits who have shared a common and extraordinary experience. I am so blessed to belong to this cocreated space of deep love, courageous honesty, and sustainable relationships.

Dear Buffalo,

We attended the Coaches Training Institute's Leadership Program together. We began as strangers. Some of us were cautious, some anxious, many open, many afraid. We learned together. We laughed together. We created an environment that encouraged us to take risks. We held each other's hands and hearts. We witnessed many transformations. And now, three years after we first met, most of us are still connected to at least one other member of our "tribe."

Some of the lessons I learned through the program included staying (commitment), speaking my truth even when it might shake things up, and that the *real* me is more compelling than my Act. In the past, I would stay in relationships and situations physically, afraid that it would mean I was a quitter if I didn't, but energetically and emotionally, I bailed. My first marriage officially ended when my ex-husband asked for a separation, but I had been separated from him emotionally and intimately for some time. I now stay fully when I am staying. In the past, I would silently allow others to speak for me even if I did not agree because I was afraid I might be rejected or ridiculed. Now I speak my truth. Sometimes, it still takes me awhile to get up my courage, but I do it eventually. This includes telling my husband I discovered his pornography use (from which he has recovered, and that led to increased closeness and commitment in our marriage), telling my son when his behavior hurts my feelings, and telling the prison project I think we're going down the martyred track and imprisoning ourselves in the process. For the most part, there is no more Sarah Act. I don't have any tolerance for myself when I am playing a role or putting on airs. It feels so much better to be me!

All of this has been huge learning and growth for me. It has shown up most in my marriage and in the Laura Whitworth Prison Project. But interestingly, I have not applied this to you Buffalo. I have been somewhat on the fringes of our tribe since before we graduated. I didn't fully believe we would have what it takes to stay together. And so I pulled away, took one foot out, rationalizing that I wouldn't feel disappointed or angry at myself for trusting when this group faded away like so many others. I didn't want to suffer from my own high expectations once again.

I felt like I cast myself into an outer circle. At least that's what I told myself. But the reality is alarmingly void of proof. I have visited four of you since we graduated and four of you while we were going through the program. And I have been in e-mail contact or phone contact with most of you at least once. Many of you have reached out to me when things were rough. Two of you have paid me for professional services. Several of you have used me as a sounding board for workshop ideas.

So it's time to come clean. My relationship with you as a group has been tainted by my lack of faith in sustainable relationships. And this tribe is proving my negative assumptions wrong. During the program, we said we were about infusing one another with courage. I did not think that would last. I looked for evidence (and found some) that I was right. But now I am looking for evidence of our staying power, and I am finding that in abundance.

I am choosing to stay, to stop playing the roles of "cautious guard of high expectations" and "commitment doubter." What does that really serve anyway? It's kept me feeling somewhat estranged. And it's given my ego a lot of food. But none of that is what I want.

So there's my confession. I'm sorry, Buffalo! I'm sorry for my disbelief in you and us. I'm sorry for my nonchalance, arrogance, and game playing. I am stepping back in fully, as one voice in the system—not *the* voice in the system, but not without a voice or a silenced voice either.

The prodigal sister has returned.

With love,
Buffalo Peace Dancer

To Papa Birch, the First Tree I Ever Hugged

I've been called a "tree hugger" because of my environmental beliefs. However, until recently, I'd never actually hugged, really embraced, a tree. It is an amazing experience.

Since I moved in with Chris, I have walked, skied, and snowshoed in our woods almost daily. These trees are my friends. They've witnessed my tears, my laughter, my friendships, my marriage, my parenting, and more. I've known that they supported me and have felt them sending me love and strength. Now I am also beginning to understand the wisdom and insights they have for me.

Dear Papa Birch,

It all started with you, that day in the woods; with Strider, my pen, and paper. What a glorious morning that was—so free, so connected to earth, self, and dog. And there you were, standing so tall and beautiful. What drew me towards you was the long scar running up your erect body. How majestic you were, proudly bearing your wound as a medal of honor, for a life lived with nobility and integrity. And I just wanted to give you a hug. As I did, the energy and the pictures that coursed through me were incredible. It felt like you were embracing me, holding me up, and showing me the way. I reached for you to tell you that I loved you and I saw you. You reached right back and told me the same. You gave me a glimpse of the power and the wisdom and the strength that lie in me, the same that is in you.

I haven't been the same since your incredible touch. I've hugged more trees since that day, and I plan to hug many more before I die. I have an idea that one of my next books will be a book of poems to the trees I've hugged. My husband will take the photos.

So thank you, Papa Birch, for the life you've lived, for the love you share, for the air we breathe, for your fine example of being deeply rooted and reaching for the sky.

Love,
Tree Hugger Sarah

To My Body

Like many North American women, I have struggled in my relationship with my body for years. I can remember dieting and worrying about how much I weighed as early as third grade. Through the years, experiencing pregnancy, yoga, illness, and an accident, I have come to love and appreciate this body of mine.

I wish I would have kept a body journal throughout my life. I think it might have mapped out a road of recovery from loathing my body to loving my body. I know there have been some pivotal moments for me, but I also believe learning to love my body has been a journey.

My wish is that people, women especially, will read this letter and become aware that a new type of relationship is possible for them with their own bodies. And perhaps this method of writing to the body will serve as a road map, returning us to appreciation and love for these most magnificent vessels we inhabit.

Dear Body,

I have been journeying with you for over thirty-eight years now. There have been times when I have loved you, times when I have hated you, proud times, disappointed times, warring times, and embarrassing times. And as I write this, I recognize that our journey is far from over. But this book of letters I'm writing is one about completing what needs completing so I can move on, in freedom.

Mostly, when I think of you, I feel a deep sense of gratitude. For the most part, you have been healthy, easy to care for, and responsive to my healthy habits and inclinations, and you have allowed me the privileges of movement, speed, flexibility, endurance, balance, a good appearance, and strength. As I begin to feel some minor effects of aging, I appreciate all the more the wondrous ways you have supported me. And I begin to recall all the ways I have mistreated you.

There were many years of disorderly eating: not eating enough, trying to vomit, overexercising, drinking diet soda, taking diet pills or other medications to flush out fat, "detoxifying," and a Candida cleanse. It was all an effort to shape you into a thin, stick-like figure so that I would feel more confident and attractive. I realize how sick this sounds now, but it was a huge part of my belief system for many years. And through all that, you never let me get way too thin, never started shutting down organs or body systems, didn't allow me to become addicted to anything, and didn't allow me to be successful at self-induced vomiting.

You have gorgeous hair, sparkling eyes, radiant coloring, energy to get through each day, a desire for healthy foods, and all your limbs and body parts including tonsils and appendix. You have run races, including a half and full marathon, competed in martial arts events, skied the half Noquemanon, hiked through Canada and northern Michigan, paddled kayaks, swam like a fish, romped with dogs, climbed up walls, leaped out of redwood trees, downhill-skied, snowshoed, ice-skated, roller-skated, rollerbladed, lifted weights, done yoga, biked (including pulling a bike trailer). You have taken down dog fencing, hauled brush, split firewood, chopped kindling, stacked firewood, and pruned trees. You have the dexterity and coordination to knit and crochet, play piano and violin, and pull out splinters and knots in children's shoe laces. You can bathe a dog and a baby. You nursed my son and birthed him, too, after carrying him in your womb for nine months. You give me the pleasure of tasting the burst of a blackberry, the feel of the wind on a hot day, the sound of laughter, the smell of my glorious wet dog on an autumn day, the sight of my son with a radiant smile on his beautiful face, the sacred joy of making love with my husband, and the soulful journey of listening to classical music.

Most recently, I experienced an accident that left me with cracked ribs. I have never broken bones before and was in a great deal of pain. I realized how active my lifestyle is. I recognized all the ways I take you, my body, for granted, moving me up and down stairs, standing over food on the stove, lifting and carrying, hugging and holding, walking my dog on a leash, laughing and coughing, breathing and walking, and even talking (which became a cardiovascular activity while I was injured). And I became amazed at how quickly you healed and responded to nurturing, rest, and compassion. Within a week I was improved enough to travel. Within two weeks, I could walk again in my woods. And within three weeks, I could even work in the garden, pulling a few weeds for a short time. I have learned to appreciate my ribs, the way they expand to allow for breathing. They protect our lungs and heart and other vital organs. They shield us. And even when they are cracked, they continue to function. And they will heal.

So many times, it's been said that we are really spirits just trapped in our bodies or living here in physical form for now. I renounce those theories. I am a body! I have a body! I love my body! I choose to inhabit this body, this incredible body that you are. I love you! When I inhabit you fully and with joy, anything is possible. Truly you are one of the most incredible gifts in my life.

Thank you, body, for serving me and for allowing me to serve you as well. I love that you delight in a bubble bath, candlelight gourmet meals, pedicures and manicures, massages and energy work—that you know you are worth any and every dollar I spend on you. Thank you for moving with joy and ease and freedom to express me fully.

Thank you, body! Thank you! Thank you! Thank you!

Your partner and friend,
Sarah

To Source

I believe that we all have a relationship to Source (God or a Higher Power) even when we say we don't believe in one. I have called myself Lutheran, Baptist, agnostic, Taoist, and pagan. Although those ideologies have shaped my relationship with Source, they are not what sustain it.

I feel very grateful to have made peace in my own mind with Source. I now believe Source created all that is and loves us dearly. And we are Source, too. We're all a part of the same energy, the same molecules.

Whether you believe something similar or something quite different, I invite you to read my letter to Source, an intimate glimpse at my relationship with Source, for the sake of possibly uncovering new awareness about your own relationship to Source.

Dear Source,

Oh my goodness! What a journey I have been on in terms of my relationship with you and my understanding of you. I can see where I have been confused. My coach calls those moments "the distortion." And for so much of my life, that's exactly where I have been, living with distorted beliefs about you. I have been caught up in language: what name you go by, who is included in the terms "Christian, chosen ones, spiritual beings, believer, enlightened people." Those things no longer matter to me.

Thank you for the "aha" moments while I was reading Eckhart Tolle's book over Christmas break 2008. I was finally able to see what I couldn't fathom before: none of the language matters. Those things I have been so easily attached to and so very much focused on don't really matter: Which path is the right one, who really knows what you want and who you are, what are we really doing here on earth, what's my purpose, who am I? Okay, it's not that they don't matter. It's just that the running around frantically trying to grasp the answers to these questions (from a place of believing that there is a "right answer" and I want to be right) was not getting me what I really wanted. I wanted a peaceful heart.

Why do I care who I am? What does it matter if I am living my purpose or not? The root of all these questions, I now see, has been a desire for peace. I want to know my place in this world, in your world, in our world. I want to feel there is someone or something bigger and wiser and more loving than I am in charge here. What a relief it is to experience the presence of the Divine!

I wish I knew what finally gave me the capacity to see what I hadn't been able to see before, hear what I was unable to hear previously, and know in my heart the inexpressible comfort and ease of trusting and knowing that you are—and I am.

In my early adulthood, I was introduced to the concept of radical grace: love, gifts, acceptance, just because, for no reason at all, especially when you feel least deserving of it. I saw how I'd associated being "good" with going to heaven and walking the spiritual path.

Now, with this new awareness, as I revisit thoughts, phrases, and Bible verses, they make sense in a whole new way. I wish I knew what made the difference. I am so, so grateful for this change in me. An old part of me would like me to feel troubled that I don't understand how it happened or what I did to make it happen (could it be it had nothing to do with me?).

Mostly, though, I accept it. Receptivity is much more powerful than I ever imagined. Grace comes when we allow it.

I understand that we must each walk the path of our own journey. Yet I feel drawn to share my journey in the hopes that it might have some relevance for someone on a similar journey. Maybe my words provide comfort to someone as they identify with the person to whom I am writing the letter. Maybe my words are a guide towards a truth they are just beginning to see. In any case, Source, I ask that as I write these letters, you take my words and filter out all that is not in the service of the highest good—anything that is only for my own glory or greed or selfish desires. Leave only that which is You speaking through me.

I thank you for your presence in my life. I know you have sheltered me from many storms, stood with me while I faced adversity, and loved me through it all. You have led me towards self-respect and self-love, which have allowed me to truly, finally, and cleanly love and respect others. I am grateful to be a part of your plan. And I humbly bring forth my piece, in your puzzle of life, that makes the whole picture clearer and potentially inspires others to bring forth their pieces of the puzzle as well.

In gratitude for the gifts I've received and in loving contribution to the expansion of our world,
Sarah

To Me from My Future Self

In my coach training, I was introduced to my "Future Self," a part of me who is about twenty years older (and wiser) than I. Through my coaching with Camilla, I have also developed a relationship with my Higher Self, the part of me who is deeply connected to Source and has my best spiritual interests at heart. This is a letter I asked my Future Self and my Higher Self to write to me and to you. I believe we are all related on a spiritual level. There's almost no difference between you and I, us and them—all the nonessential melts away. And we are just heart essence to heart essence.

Here's a message from my—our—heart essence.

Dear Sarah and Others on the Journey of Life,

Bless you for choosing to inhabit bodies and live this life now. You are living in a time of great turbulence and tremendous opportunity. You have chosen to come here to learn and grow. You have also chosen to come here to heal and give. In everything, there is balance: both giving and receiving.

Think about what drew you to this process and, for readers, what drew you to this book. This is a large part of who you are—a curious seeker, exploring, discovering wisdom along the way. Start having the conversations that matter. Share what you are learning. Seek the answers to your questions. Seek relationships with others who are on the path of learning, loving, and remembering who we are.

As you awake to your essential selves, you will notice and find others who are waking up as well. Stay connected. Even when people forget their divinity momentarily and hurt you, stay connected to the truth of who you are and the truth of who they are. Look for ways to gently remind yourself and others of what really matters.

There is so much support for your journey. If you had any idea of the number of beings who surround you every day, keeping you safe, sending you good energy, rooting for your learning, your growing, and your responding with love to yourself and to others in each and every moment, you'd be absolutely amazed.

Go then, and live this life to the best of your abilities. Help others live their best lives as well. Experience the joy that is present. Find the good in everything. Create your "happily ever after"—now. Know that you are good and so are others. Speak your truth, and let others speak theirs.

Blessings to you, dear one(s)!

Love,
Your Future, Higher, and Spiritual Self (Selves)

Appendices

Questions for Reflection

To Little Sarah, a Letter to Myself

1. What's your relationship like with yourself?
2. If you wrote a letter to yourself, what would be the main themes? Self-love? Self-pity? Self-criticism? Something else?
3. What do you want your relationship with yourself to be like?
4. What's the first step?

To South Korea, Place of My Birth

1. Where were you born, and what relationship do you have with that place?
2. What does it mean to have roots someplace?
3. What does it mean to be given wings?

To My Birth Mother

1. What's your experience with adoption, mothering, or loss of a primary adult figure in your life?
2. What does this letter stir up in you?
3. What would you need to say in order to be complete with your relationship with your biological mom, whether she is still living or not?

To the First Home I Remember

1. Where was your first home, and how do you think about it?
2. What one place from your childhood might you like to revisit? Why?
3. If walls could talk, what might they say?

To Molly, My Sister

1. When have you seen someone through the eyes of jealousy?

2. What's at the root of (your) sibling rivalry?

3. What's possible from a place of deep understanding (both of you and of the other person)?

To Chad, My First Love

1. Who was your first love? How do you feel about this person now?

2. Who was the one who got away? What story have you made up about that relationship?

3. If you weren't afraid, what might you be willing to do in either of these relationships?

To the Cedar Falls Bullies

1. When was a time you have been the "victim"?

2. When was a time you have been the "perpetrator"?

3. How are each of these roles limiting?

4. How do we break free?

To Martha, My First Music Teacher

1. Who in your life was a model of patience and understanding?

2. Who might you see differently today than you did when you were a child?

3. What would it mean to you to have someone from your past let you know how deeply you had touched their life?

To My Aunt Heidi, Role Model of Forgiveness

1. Who in your life has forgiven you or showed great understanding when your behavior was less than ideal?

2. When have you been the one to forgive?

3. If your behaviors are setting a pattern or "teaching through example" for others, what are they learning from you? Is this the kind of behavior you intend to model for future interactions?

To the People of Greenwood

1. Where have you been focused on a certain group or person seeing you a certain way?
2. How has this been inauthentic?
3. What price have you and they paid for this behavior?

To Mr. Navrestad, My Band Director

1. Who has touched your life deeply but might not know it?
2. What keeps you from reaching out in loving service?
3. What allows us to forgive ourselves when we can't ask forgiveness from someone who is dead?

To St. Olaf College

1. What experience have you had (possibly educational) that you did not fully appreciate at the time but have now come to be grateful for?
2. What did you need as a young adult that a learning institution could have provided?
3. What would you say to a young adult who wanted to drop out of school to get married or work full-time?

To Pinstripes Petites

1. How does the definition of "justification" strike you?
2. What's the relationship between apologies, forgiveness, and making amends?
3. What event in your past lurks in your shadows?

To Me on the Day of My First Wedding

1. If there's a choice you regret in your life, how much compassion do you have for the part of you that made that decision?
2. What would it be like to have a conversation with a younger you?
3. What would you say to yourself? What might that self say to you?

To Margie and Bill, My Ex-Parents-in-Law

1. How are you different when you're in "fear mode"?

2. What situations make you feel especially vulnerable?

3. What might it be like to be okay being imperfect, messy, raw, and real?

To Lake Tainter, My "Happy Place"

1. Where is your "happy place"?

2. What gifts might nature be trying to give you?

3. When will you take a moment to receive all that is being offered to you?

To Angie and Brian, My Former Foster Children

1. When have you agreed to something based on an ideal vision and then discovered the reality to be quite different from what you had in mind?

2. How can we create systems that support people and families who are struggling?

3. What makes it possible for us to forgive ourselves when we have greatly wronged another?

To Me, the One Who Gave Birth

1. What have you struggled to birth in your life?

2. What wants to be born right now?

3. What gets in your way?

4. What supports you?

To the Ya Yas

1. If you have a group of friends like this, what similarities do you see? If you don't, what interests you about this group?

2. How is your life different (or how would it be different) because of the support of friends like these?

3. Who do you need to be in order to have sacred connections to others?

To Chris and Jen on Moon Mountain

1. Whom in your life were you once close with but now have a strained or distant relationship with?

2. What has been your story about what happened?

3. What do you imagine their story might be?

4. What's a new story that wants to emerge?

To Ann, a Woman in an Emotionally Abusive Relationship

1. What's a big mistake in your life, and how often does it haunt you?

2. How much responsibility do you believe we have for the welfare of those we love and care about? For strangers?

3. How do we balance forgiving ourselves and calling ourselves forth to something better?

To Christopher on the Day of Our Wedding

1. What qualities do you value in your primary relationship? Or what qualities are you seeking in a potential partner?

2. In the romantic story of your life, what chapter are you living right now?

3. What does "happily ever after" look like for you?

To Nancy, My Husband's Ex-Wife

1. How do you think and feel about people from your spouse's past?

2. What relationship do you see between your current primary relationships and any unhealed parts from past relationships?

3. Where in your life might one relationship be affecting the quality of another?

To Anna and Jesse, My Husband's Children

1. Whom have you rejected because you felt rejected by them?

2. When did you become so hurt that you couldn't hear or see the other person anymore?

3. What does it take to throw off the trap of "victim" and reempower yourself in a relationship?

To a Former Colleague Who Owns a Pornography Business

1. What's a hot topic for you, something that usually pushes your buttons?

2. What would it be like to sit with it, as I described in this letter, breathing in the difficult feelings that go with this situation and exhaling a wish or intention?

3. When do you find yourself judging others? What helps you remember we are all in this together?

To Karen Kimsey-House,
President and CEO of the Coaches Training Institute

1. What organization or company has had a big impact on you? How so?
2. What kind of letter would you write to the president of this organization?
3. What kind of leader, CEO, or president would you be or are you? What do you create for others?

To Camilla, My Coach, My Spiritual Guide, My Friend

1. What is your life like because you have a Camilla in it? Or what would your life be like if you had this kind of relationship with this kind of person?
2. Who might you need to be to attract her into your life?
3. How far away are you from being this kind of person yourself? What will draw you closer?

To the Women of Denver Women's Correctional Facility

1. How do you imprison yourself?
2. What does freedom mean to you?
3. Who do you know who might need a nudge to see their potential and begin to shine?
4. What are you willing to do about it?

To the Buffalo, My Leadership Tribe

1. Who is your tribe?
2. What role do you typically play in your tribe?
3. What would it be like to see this tribe and yourself in a new way?
4. What might be possible for you and your tribe from this new viewpoint?

To Papa Birch, the First Tree I Ever Hugged

1. How have you connected with a special plant, animal, or mineral?
2. What gifts have you received from this connection?
3. If trees could talk, what do you think they'd say?

To My Body

1. What is your current relationship with your body?
2. What kind of relationship would you like to have with your body?
3. What might your body need from you in order to be its healthiest and happiest?

To Source

1. How would you describe your relationship with God, Source, etc.?
2. How does this relationship affect your life?
3. What kind of relationship do you want to have with God?

To Me from My Future Self

1. How easy is it for you to accept this message as truth?
2. What happens to any resistance you have when you choose to soften and allow?
3. How might you live differently if you took this message to heart?

To Those Wanting to Follow This Letter-Writing Journey

I first set out to write these letters for myself, and then I decided to share them. At some point in the process, I became very concerned about the content of some of my letters and their potentially negative impact on readers. My coach encouraged me to at least consider offering the process if not the specific letters.

Although I am choosing to share most of the letters I wrote this past year, I am also choosing to share the process itself. I believe I stumbled across and created a "map" for the journey of life. And so I have outlined my steps, including alternatives I considered and questions I asked.

I encourage you to use my process as a skeletal foundation for your own discoveries, your own journey. Then give yourself permission to explore what turns up for you.

I have already begun writing a companion book with more guidance for this process. I imagine it will be like an interactive journal.

Dear Letter Writer,

I bless you on the journey you are intending to go on. For me it has been an incredible process of self-discovery, self-growth, self-awareness, and self-love. I hope that your experience is as enlightening, enjoyable, and worthwhile as mine was.

Here is my recollection of the steps I followed (or planned and deviated from):

1. Made a chronological list (bucket list) of potential letters.
2. Followed the energy of which one seemed to call to me, to want to be written—about one to two each week.
3. Stayed with a letter until the energy waned—sometimes completed a first draft, sometimes worked with ideas to include, sometimes only got a few paragraphs and then felt called to another letter.
4. Read my letter to my biological mom out loud twice.
5. Started looking at the technical aspects: publishing, FSC-certified printer, etc.
6. Set specific times when I'd work on the letters.
7. Began sharing more letters out loud.
8. Began editing for higher and higher levels of truth telling.
9. Revised them from Higher Self perspective.
10. Wrote introductions and added questions to consider.
11. Worked with the order (table of contents).
12. Looked for themes.
13. Got stuck around some of the more difficult letters—ones in which I was asking for forgiveness. Journaled on it and received wisdom from my Higher Self. *(See letter on page 135.)*
14. Revised based on Inner Voice.
15. Had coaching session on process with Camilla. Focused on process: making a map for others versus quality of the letters themselves.
16. Had creativity consultation with Helen after a writing workshop: wisdom from journaling (heart stone message). *(See letter on page 136.)*
17. Brainstormed possibilities: where to go from here.
    a. "Coming Clean"–themed sharing with Indigo Wild soap samples
    b. Process only book
    c. Publish book with questions
    d. Workshops
18. Went back and recorded myself reading all the letters; paid attention to what felt clean (literally, mentally, and emotionally). Listened to self, and edited based on that—truthfulness and no ego.

19. Wrote process letter.
20. Ran a spell check.
21. Printed for style editor.
22. Reviewed suggestions and made changes.
23. Went back through, moved questions to the end, and deleted some letters that either didn't go with the chronology or didn't feel true anymore.
24. Asked husband to take photos for cover. Sent photos to book designer/editor.
25. Sent manuscript file to editor.
26. Sent paper files to people I asked for endorsements.
27. Sent electronic file to Jon for "box testing."
28. Sent letters to people for whom they were intended.
29. Received editing comments via track changes in review.
30. Made revisions.
31. Worked with printer on page count and pricing.
32. Worked with book designer/editor on cover art, fonts, numbering, etc.
33. Received print file from book designer/editor.
34. Sent to printer.
35. Celebrated!

* * *

Letter from Higher Self during time when I doubted that I had the courage to share these parts of my past publicly:

She says, "You aren't in charge here. You don't get to decide why you're here or what to write or how to be used. When you're in the flow, there is no choice. There is grace. There is ease. There is a letting go and allowing. Letting go of relationships—you have such an overly responsible notion about relationships. You read these letters, and you think it's entirely your fault. Oh honey! We are each just doing our best. Sure, your mind knew better. Sure, your heart constricted. Yes, you hurt children. The hurt child in you lashed out at hurting children—of course she did. Heal her. Love her up. Forgive her. There's really nothing to forgive—ever—forgiveness is a concept born out of a shame-and-blame culture. It actually has little use (other than a stepping stone towards self-healing when needed). Everything happens for a reason. When we're unconscious, we're simply playing out the script that society, our parents, our personality, and others write/wrote for us. Once we're awake, that's when life begins. So write your letters, or don't. But wake up, and stay awake! Know where the current of Source love is flowing, and jump. That's the only choice you really have to make. This is the letter from your Future Self, encouraging you to complete the book, go through the process. You can decide each step (staying on the current of Source love), whether to have them printed, and whether to make them available to anyone other than whom you're willing to give them to. The world does need them. But Source will take care of that. You decide if you want to be the one to bring them. You're right. There will be consequences. Some might be pleasant, some not. Is that what matters most to you? Can you live with whatever consequences come for the sake of offering a gift to the world—a gift they may choose to receive or not? You can't be partially riding the love current and partially not: you'll be torn in shreds. You still bear scars from major whiplash from leaping on and being thrown off. Because your fear isn't aligned with the love vibe, you can't hang on. You know the world needs this process as much as you needed this process. You won't keep it from them. Whether or not they accept it from you, you're willing to offer it. Willingness to risk rejection, to offer what you see as valuable, to face whatever consequences come, to be well-used by Source of love, is the vibe needed to launch you onto the love current and keep you there."

* * *

Letter from Heart Stone Journaling:

Beautiful, loving Sarah,

You have gone the distance with these letters. You heard the call. You answered, with willingness, creativity, and compassion. You continued, staying the course even when faced with the turbulence of uncomfortable memories and challenging publication scenarios. It is now time to listen to your spirit. What would feed your spirit here? What would complete or bring this process to completion? "I want a once-over. They're so close. Many were written with great love. Some were written with extreme honesty in mind." Honesty and courage are good. These were absolutely areas that you needed to grow, push yourself. You have developed your truth-telling muscle. You are well on your way there. *And* what your heart, this heart, wants you to know is that love is courageous. Radical, transformational, true love, free love, no strings attached, no mess, clean and clear, pure love takes courage and honesty. Thank you for bringing that to the process, and now return to your heart. Look over these letters one more time with a centered, peaceful heart. From there, share the process; use it as one of the maps you explore next year on your journey. Have it edited or published, if that's the form this map, these letters, want to take. You are complete as you are. The letters are almost as complete as you—this is the last 5K of the marathon. Hang in there. Stay the course. Trust the journey. The last quarter is yet to be revealed.

Love,
Heart Stone at Joy Center

* * *

Now you've seen the fruits of my journey and received a "behind the scenes" glimpse of what it entailed for me as well. Go forth, write your own letters, seek your own inner wisdom, and heal your own uncomfortable places. May Source bless you with the courage to keep looking and the willingness to respond in love to yourself and others, no matter what.

Bon voyage on your letter-writing journey!

Love,
Sarah

Founded in 2007, Eco-Libris is a green company that works with book readers, publishers, authors, bookstores and others in the book industry to balance out the paper used for books by planting trees. More than 30 million trees are cut down annually for virgin paper used for the production of books sold in the U.S. alone. Eco-Libris aims to raise awareness to the environmental impacts of using paper for the production of books and provide people and businesses with an affordable and easy way to do something about it: plant one tree for every book they read, sell or publish.

Customers also receive a sticker made of recycled paper for every book they balance out saying "One tree planted for this book" and can later display these stickers on their books' sleeves.

Eco-Libris partners with three highly respected U.S. and U.K. registered non-profit organizations that work in collaboration with local communities in developing countries to plant these trees. These trees are planted in high ecological and sustainable standards in Latin America (Nicaragua, Guatemala, Panama, Belize, Honduras) and Africa (Malawi), where deforestation is a crucial problem. Planting trees in these places not only helps to fight climate change and conserve soil and water, but also benefits many local people, for whom these trees offer many benefits, such as improvement of crops and additional food and income, and an opportunity for a better future.

So far Eco-Libris has planted with its planting partners more than 120,000 trees.

For more information on Eco-Libris, please visit its website, http://www.ecolibris.net, and blog, http://ecolibris.blogspot.com.